Rate Risk
MANAGEMENT

**FIXED
INCOME
STRATEGIES
USING
FUTURES
OPTIONS
AND
SWAPS**

George D.
Oberhofer

PROBUS PUBLISHING COMPANY
CHICAGO, ILLINOIS

This publication is designed to provide accurate and
authoritative information in regard to the subject matter covered. It is sold with the understanding that the
publisher is not engaged in rendering legal, accounting
or other professional service. If legal advice or other
expert assistance is required, the services of a compe-
tent professional person should be sought.

FROM A DECLARATION OF PRINCIPLES JOINTLY ADOPTED BY A
COMMITTEE OF THE AMERICAN BAR ASSOCIATION AND A COM-
MITTEE OF PUBLISHERS.

Library of Congress Cataloging in Publication Data

Oberhofer, George D.
    Rate risk management.

    Includes index.
        1. Futures. 2. Options (Finance) I. Title.
HG6024.A3024   1988   332.64′4   88-12603
ISBN 1-55738-004-X

Printed in the United States of America

1 2 3 4 5 6 7 8 9 0

To George and Leonard

Contents

Acknowledgments

Many of the concepts and strategies explained in this book are based on the insights of the author's customers and colleagues at the Chicago Corporation. In particular, the author wishes to express gratitude to Richard Robb and to Robert Rudolph: the former for sharing his clarity and rigor of thought; and the latter for providing a work environment conducive to creativity.

Introduction

Presenting a truly comprehensive examination of all aspects of rate risk management in a single volume is a formidable task. Entire books can be written on each of the topics examined in this book. Advances in our theoretical understanding of the determination of interest rates and the behavior of options will continue to occur at a steady rate. Innovation in the design of new futures, swap, and option products also continues rapidly. Even a text which at this moment presented an exhaustive study of rate risk management would in five years be in large part obsolete.

The objectives of this book are more modest: to provide the reader with an intuitive grasp of basic risk management concepts and techniques and to provide the analytical tools required to implement basic risk management techniques in a sound fashion. The risk manager who wishes to use the most sophisticated techniques now available may still need to consult specialists in those techniques to apply them properly. Still, if by applying the concepts presented here the risk manager can distinguish valid from spurious strategies among the many strategies available in the marketplace, he will have gained much.

This book is organized to move the reader from basic, intuitive concepts to the mathematical embodiment of those concepts, and then to the detailed application of those concepts in practical rate risk management situations.

Chapter 1 explains the definition and measurement of rate risk, starting from the concept of a rate of return and the relationship between the rate, price, and time to maturity of a fixed income security. Two basic risk measurement yardsticks—*duration* and *basis point value*—are presented; these two measurement tools are used throughout the rest of the text. A third tool—*slope point value*—is discussed as a means to measure the effect of nonparallel shifts of the yield curve.

Chapter 2 introduces the concept of a *forward security* and shows that futures contracts on fixed income securities are specialized types of forward securities. Two other concepts—*the pricing principle* and *arbitrage*—are also introduced which together explain the relationship between futures and cash securities.

The first part of Chapter 3 describes the conventions used in the design of futures contracts and their effects on futures pricing. The second part lists in detail information which is pertinent to using and understanding each of today's most important fixed income futures contracts.

Chapter 4 provides examples of how futures can be used in rate risk management to protect asset value, stabilize return, and stabilize a cost of funds. In addition, examples are presented which illustrate *cross-hedging*, where some characteristics of hedged items differ substantially from those of the futures used to hedge.

Chapter 5 introduces the concept of interest rate swaps as an alternative to futures and shows how swap interest sensitivity can be analyzed in terms of basis point value and slope point value.

Chapter 6 introduces the concept of options. It first views options on a strictly intuitive level, to give the reader a good feel for option price behavior. Then, using easily understandable arbitrage arguments and certain assumptions, it develops a mathematical model of option price behavior, which is the mechanical equivalent of the Black-Scholes option pricing formula. Finally, it shows how the Black-Scholes model can be derived without making uncomfortable assumptions about risk preference or prediction of returns.

Chapter 7 describes the conventions used in the design of

option contracts on futures and lists pertinent information about today's major futures option contracts.

Chapter 8 shows how the use of option concepts and option contracts enables a risk manager to hedge securities and products with embedded option features. It discusses the pros and cons of such strategies as delta-neutral hedging, call writing, and portfolio insurance. It also describes the principles needed to analyze and hedge mortgage-backed securities, commitments, caps, and collars.

CHAPTER 1

Rate Sensitivity Defined and Measured

Overview

As finance professionals, we are in the business of rate risk management—finding investments that will yield the greatest expected profit for a given level of risk; or conversely, the least risk for a given expected profit. Futures, swaps, and options are superb tools for rate risk management. Before we can use them, we must be able to define and measure rate risk. This chapter introduces the concepts and techniques needed to analyze the rate sensitivity of many cash assets or liabilities. The insights provided are also fundamental to the use of futures, swaps, or options, as will be seen in later chapters.

Investors buy financial assets, such as Treasury or corporate securities, because the cash payments which will result from ownership are expected to be greater than the cost of purchasing and holding the security, or because the expected payment pattern meets specific cashflow needs. The price an investor is willing to pay depends on the rate at which the security is expected to increase the owner's wealth (its rate of return) and on the degree of risk that the security will not result in the anticipated cashflows. In the marketplace, a given security is traded until the remaining prospective buyers place slightly less value on the security than the remaining prospective sellers. Thereafter, trades occur at a price between the most eager buyer's bid and the most eager seller's offered price.

Rate, Price, and Maturity

The simplest security is one which promises to pay the owner a single, known lump sum of cash one period in the future and which will make the promised payment without fail, e.g., a one-year Treasury bill. The following formula describes the relationship between the amount of the lump sum, the rate of return investors require, and the value they place on the security:

$$\text{Value} = \frac{\text{lump sum payment}}{1 + \text{required rate of return}}$$

or

$$P = \frac{F}{(1 + r)} \qquad (1\text{-}1)$$

where

    P = Market value or price of the security

    F = Amount of promised lump sum or face value of the security at its maturity

    r = Rate of return in one period.

This follows because investors insist on receiving not only P, but some additional amount $(r \times P)$ in return for their initial investment calculated as follows:

$$F = P \times (1 + r).$$

An investor in the simple security receives no coupon or cash payments before maturity and so earns the required return solely from the difference between the initial price and the face value received at maturity. Such securities are always bought and sold at a discount from their face values and are referred to as *pure discount securities*.

Suppose an investor requires a return of r per period and is evaluating a pure discount security with two periods to maturity. To receive a return, or interest rate, per year of r on the security for two years, the investor must receive

$$[P \times (1 + r)] \times (1 + r)$$

at maturity. The security will be valued at

$$P = \frac{F}{(1 + r)^2}.$$

In general, for a security with N periods to maturity,

$$P = \frac{F}{(1 + r)^N}. \qquad (1\text{-}2a)$$

we can rearrange Equation 1-2 to determine the value of each variable, given the others:

$$F = P \times (1 + r)^N \qquad (1\text{-}2b)$$

$$r = (F/P)^{(1/N)} - 1 \qquad (1\text{-}2c)$$

$$N = \frac{\ln (F/P)}{\ln (1 + r)}. \qquad (1\text{-}2d)$$

If F refers to the price at which a security is sold, and N to the time between purchase and sale, Equation 1-2c can be used to infer the rate earned given the purchase (P) and sale (F) prices of a security if it is sold before maturity.

These relationships apply when the rate of return is calculated with the assumption that returns are reinvested once per year or compounded annually. Appendix 1 discusses in detail the effects of different compounding periods and straight-line or simple rate calculations.

Default Risk versus Rate Risk

The simple, pure discount security discussed so far is assumed to pay its face value at maturity *without fail*. There is no chance of failure to pay or default, and in this sense the security is riskless. Indeed, for the buyer of the security whose sole objective is to earn rate r until maturity, the security is riskless. However, a different kind of risk confronts the investor who intends to hold the security for a while, then sell it before maturity. The risk is that the the rate of return the market requires of the security will change during the time it is held. If the investor buys a one-year, $100 face-value security and the market rate of return is 10%, the investor pays:

$$\frac{\$100}{(1 + .10)} = \$90.91$$

for the security. After six months, the investor expects to sell the security for a price of

$$\frac{\$100}{(1 + .10)^{.5}} = \$95.35.$$

The investor earns

$$\frac{\$95.35^{(1/.5)}}{\$90.91} - 1 = .10, \text{ or } 10\%$$

annualized for the six-month holding period, as expected. However, if the market rate rises from 10 to 11% during the holding period, the investor will be able to sell the security for only

$$\frac{\$100}{1.11^{.5}} = \$94.92,$$

and will earn only

$$\frac{\$94.92^{(1/.5)}}{\$90.91} - 1 = .09, \text{ or } 9\%.$$

A more violent shift in rates may even cause the investor to lose money on the investment. The degree to which a change in the market rate will lead to a change in the value of an investor's assets is called *rate risk,* or, more accurately, *rate sensitivity.* The market value of the one-year bill is sensitive to rate changes, but would not pose rate risk to an investor with an objective of earning 10% for one year.

Rate Sensitivity Measured: Duration

A closer look at the price/rate/maturity relationship enables us to predict almost perfectly how a given change in rates will change price.

If we express the change in rates, Δr, as a fraction of $(1 + r)$ and the change in price, ΔP, as a fraction of P, then:

$$\frac{\Delta r}{(1 + r)} \times D = -\frac{\Delta P}{P}. \tag{1-3}$$

The value D directly links the percentage change in $(1 + r)$ to the resultant percentage change in P. Risk managers refer to D as *duration,* since for a pure discount security

$$\text{duration} = \text{time to maturity}$$

or

$$D = N. \qquad (1\text{-}4)$$

The accuracy and usefulness of duration as a measure of security rate sensitivity can be illustrated with a simple example. Let's assume that two securities have a final value of $1 million and a market rate of 10%. One security matures in one year and the other in five years. What is the effect of a .01% or one basis point increase in rates?

At the 10% rate the values of the securities are:

$N = 1$ $\qquad\qquad\qquad\qquad\qquad$ $N = 5$

$$\frac{\$1,000,000}{1.10^1} = \$909,090.91 \qquad \frac{\$1,000,000}{1.10^5} = \$620,921.32$$

By rearranging Equation 1-3, we can use duration to predict the change in the prices of both securities.

$$-P \times \frac{\Delta r}{(1 + r)} \times D = \Delta P$$

For $N = 1$, $\$909,091 \times \dfrac{.0001}{(1.10)} \times 1 = \$82.64$, and

for $N = 5$, $\$620,921 \times \dfrac{.0001}{(1.10)} \times 5 = \$282.24$.

Using the price formula (Equation 1-2a) to calculate the change in the prices of the securities' prices which results from a one basis point rate change, we can duplicate the results obtained using duration.

For $N = 1$,

$$\frac{\$1,000,000}{1.10^1} - \frac{\$1,000,000}{1.1001^1} = \$82.64, \text{ and}$$

for $N = 5$,

$$\frac{\$1,000,000}{1.10^5} - \frac{\$1,000,000}{1.1001^5} = \$282.24.$$

From Duration to Dollars: Basis Point Value

In the last example we used both duration and direct calculation to determine the dollar change in price resulting from a .01% or one basis point change in rates. The resulting predicted price change is known as a *basis point value*, often abbreviated as BPV.

BPV = dollar change in security price for a .01% change in rate.

Basis point value, even more than duration, is the basic tool to use in rate sensitivity management. As seen above, BPV can be inferred from duration:

$$BPV = -P \times \frac{.0001}{(1 + r)} \times D \qquad (1\text{-}5)$$

or calculated directly:

$$BPV = \frac{F}{(1 + r - .00005)^N} - \frac{F}{(1 + r + .00005)^N}. \qquad (1\text{-}6)$$

Note that in Equation 1-6, a one basis point change in r is made by first raising, then lowering r by one-half basis point. The distinction between this method and the one used in the previous example (where the market rate was simply raised by one full basis point) is small in practical terms; however, it theoretically provides a more neutral prediction of rate sensitivity, regardless of the direction of the rate change.

Advantages of BPV in Rate Risk Management

It is obvious from Equations 1-5 and 1-6 that duration and basis point value are intimately related, and that it is a simple matter to convert from one to the other. However, BPV is often a more useful rate risk measurement tool for three reasons:

1. BPV is concrete. It expresses interest sensitivity in dollars and cents rather than abstractly, as does duration.
2. BPV requires no context to be interpreted correctly. To understand fully the meaning of a security's duration, you must

also know its market value and rate. BPV summarizes in a single number the effect of all three.

3. BPV is calculated conveniently using automatic functions commonly designed into financial calculators. These automatic functions cannot be used to calculate duration directly; BPV must be calculated first as an intermediate step.

Accuracy of Price Change Predictions

In theory, BPV and duration provide perfectly accurate measures of price sensitivity only for very small rate changes. As seen in Equation 1-5, a given price change is a function not only of the size of a change in rates, but also of the overall level of rates at the time of the change. A large enough change in rates changes the level of rates as well, rendering the price change predicted by duration less accurate for large moves in rates. In practice, the rate sensitivity predicted duration is quite satisfactory for rate changes of even 50 basis points or so.

In addition, duration and BPV measurements are perfectly accurate only for a short period of time after the measurements are made. The duration of a nine–month pure discount bill is .75, but after three months will have shrunk to .50. The initial duration measurement (or corresponding BPV) is rendered inaccurate simply as a result of the passage of time. The shorter the life of a security, the larger a portion of that life is represented by the passage of a week; thus BPV shrinks in percentage terms more rapidly for short–term than for long–term securities.

Duration and measurements, then, are not constants for a given security. They should be recalculated periodically to compensate for the passage of time and for changes in the level of rates.

Portfolios of Pure Discount Securities

An investor may hold a portfolio of pure discount securities and may wish to evaluate the interest sensitivity of the entire portfolio. The value of this portfolio is the sum of the values of its components:

$$\text{Portfolio Value} = \frac{F_1}{(1 + r)^{N_1}} + \frac{F_2}{(1 + r)^{N_2}} + \cdots + \frac{F_P}{(1 + r)^{N_P}}$$

where

$F_1 \ldots F_P$ = Face values of securities 1 through P

$N_1 \ldots N_P$ = Times to maturity of securities 1 through P.

Similarly, the basis point value of the portfolio is the sum of the basis point values of its components:

$$\text{Portfolio BPV} = \text{BPV}_1 + \text{BPV}_2 + \cdots + \text{BPV}_P \qquad (1\text{-}7)$$

where

$\text{BPV}_1 \ldots \text{BPV}_P$ = basis point values of securities 1 through P.

The duration of a portfolio of pure discount securities is more difficult to calculate. The duration of a portfolio equals the market value weighted average of the maturities of its securities:

$$D = \frac{(P_1 \times N_1) + (P_2 \times N_2) + \cdots + (P_P \times N_P)}{P_1 + P_2 + P_3 + \cdots + P_P} \qquad (1\text{-}8)$$

where

$P_1 \ldots P_P$ = the market prices of securities 1 through p.

An approximate duration may also be backed out of the BPV formula:

$$D = \frac{\text{BPV}}{P} \times \frac{1 + r}{.0001} \qquad (1\text{-}9)$$

where

BPV = the total BPV of the portfolio.

Rate Sensitivity for Coupon Securities

The niceties of price and interest sensitivity calculations for pure discount securities would be of limited benefit if they could not be applied to coupon-bearing securities, which comprise a large fraction of the securities held by investors. Fortunately, the concepts used to analyze pure discount securities are the building blocks used to analyze the more complex, coupon-bearing securities.

Consider a four–year bond with a face value of $100 and a coupon of $10 paid in one installment at the end of each year. The stream of cash payments in this bond is as follows:

Now	1 Year	2 Years	3 Years	4 Years
$0	$10	$10	$10	$110

The pattern of cashflows associated with this coupon bond is the same as the cashflow pattern of a portfolio of pure discount securities. Three of the pure discount securities pay $10 after one, two, and three years, respectively. The fourth pays $110 after four years. As in the case of a portfolio of pure discount securities, the value of this coupon bond is the sum of the values of its components. If the required return is 10%, the bond is worth

$$P = \frac{\$10}{1.10^1} + \frac{\$10}{1.10^2} + \frac{\$10}{1.10^3} + \frac{\$110}{1.10^4}$$

$$= \$9.09 + \$8.26 + \$7.52 + \$75.13 = \$100.$$

The basis point value of this bond is likewise the sum of the basis point values of its component cashflows:

$$BPV = \$9.09 \times \frac{.0001}{1.10} \times 1 + \ \$8.26 \times \frac{.0001}{1.10} \times 2 +$$

$$\$7.52 \times \frac{.0001}{1.10} \times 3 + \$75.13 \times \frac{.0001}{1.10} \times 4 = \$.0317.$$

The duration of uhe bond is the value-weighted average time to receipt of its component cashflows:

$$D = \frac{\$9.09 \times 1 + \$8.26 \times 2 + \$7.52 \times 3 + \$75.13 \times 4}{\$100} = 3.49.$$

Equation 1-9 yields almost the same result:

$$D = \frac{\$.0317}{\$100} \times \frac{1 + .10}{.0001} = 3.49 \text{ years.}$$

Reflecting on this example yields important insights into the nature of interest sensitivity for coupon securities. The duration of this security is less than its time to maturity. The higher the coupon of a coupon-bearing note or bond, the shorter its duration relative to its time to final maturity, since duration is a value-weighted average time to receipt of all cashflows, not just the final cashflow.

Nonetheless, the basis point value of a high-coupon security will be larger than that of a low-coupon security, given the same face value and maturity date for both, even though the duration of the higher coupon security will be smaller. This is because the current market value of the higher coupon security will be larger; both duration and market value play a role in the determination of BPV.

Finally, a security with given coupon, face value, and maturity date will have a lower basis point value when market rates are high than when market rates are low. Higher rates imply lower-market value; further, an increase in market rates will diminish the market value of distant cash flows more than the market value of nearby cash flows, shifting the value weighting toward the nearby cash flows, and shrinking duration.

Extended Applications of Duration and Basis Point Value

To the extent that the size and timing of cash flows can be determined, the BPV and duration of any kind of financial asset may be calculated. Bank loans, corporate bonds, and commercial mortgages all result in a more or less predictable series of cash payments, which can be analyzed as if they were separate, pure-discount securities.

Debts and liabilities can be analyzed using the same set of tools. A bond sold by a corporation can be viewed as a negative asset owned by that corporation. If the bond's required return rises, the value of that bond, and hence the value of the bond-holder's claim against the firm, is reduced. The price, BPV, or duration of a liability is calculated just as if it were an asset, realizing, of course, that a decline in the value of a liability is a benefit, not a cost, to the liability issuer.

The last class of securities to be examined is variable-rate securities. As an example, consider a loan to a corporation of $100. The corporation pays interest on the loan at a rate which is to be adjusted quarterly. Principal, as well as all accrued interest on the loan, will be paid back in a single lump sum at the end of five years. The rate of interest on the loan has just been set at 10%. At first glance, the loan appears to be a pure discount security with a duration of five years and a BPV of roughly 4.5 cents. However, if interest rates rise, the rate at which interest accrues on the loan will be increased at the end of the quarter to the pre-vailing market rate. In effect, the debt up until then will be retired and replaced immediately by a new debt, with interest to be paid at the new market rate. The maturity of the debt, as far as rate risk is concerned, is only one quarter of a year; the duration is .25 and the BPV is roughly 0.23 cents. A $100 floating rate debt, repriced daily, has a duration of 1/365 year and a BPV of .00249 cents, even though the loan legally might be classified as perpetual.

Rate Sensitivity of a Balance Sheet

Basis point value may also be used to measure the interest sen-sitivity of an entire balance sheet or portfolio of assets and the liabilities which fund them. To do so, calculate the basis point value of each asset and liability on the balance sheet. Add up the BPVs of all the assets, and subtract from this total the BPVs of all of the liabilities. (Exclude equity from the calculation.) The net result will be the basis point value of the entire balance sheet. If the balance sheet BPV is positive, the balance sheet behaves like an asset, losing value (of equity) as rates rise. If the BPV is nega-tive, the balance sheet behaves like a liability, and equity value will rise as rates rise.

Limitations of Basis Point Value or Duration

Three important caveats must be noted by the user of BPV and duration in any of the applications discussed above:

1. Duration and BPV are accurate measures of rate sensitivity only for relatively small changes in rates. BPV and duration should be recalculated to adjust for the effects of significant rate shifts.
2. The BPV and duration of securities will change over time as their time to maturity changes. They should be recalculated to adjust for the passage of time.
3. BPV and duration are perfectly accurate measures of rate risk for pure discount securities; however, they are accurate measures only of the effect of a uniform, additive, or parallel shift in the rates for all components of a portfolio, coupon security, or balance sheet. If the market rates for different components change by different amounts, the effect on

market value will not be predicted perfectly by BPV or duration.

The Effects of Nonparallel Rate Shifts

The relationship between market rates on various securities and their respective times to maturity is called the *term structure* or *yield curve*. A flat yield curve with market rates for all maturities equal to 10% is illustrated in Figure 1-1.

Consider two securities—I and II—in a market characterized by the yield curve in Figure 1-1.

Year	Rate	I Cashflow	I Present Value	II Cashflow	II Present Value
1	.10				
2	.10			$82.64	$68.30
3	.10				
4	.10	$200.00	$136.60		
5	.10				
6	.10			$121.00	$68.30
Totals:		$200.00	$136.60	$203.64	$136.60
Duration:		4		4	
BPV:		$.0497		$.0497	

The market value, duration, and basis point value of I and II are identical. Yet, observe the effect of a nonparallel shift in rates:

Year	Rate	I Cashflow	I Present Value	II Cashflow	II Present Value
1	.085				
2	.09			$82.64	$69.56
3	.095				
4	.10	$200.00	$136.60		
5	.105				
6	.11			$121.00	$64.69
Totals:		$200.00	$136.60	$203.64	$134.25
Duration:		4		3.92	
BPV:		$.0497		$.0477	
Change:		$0		$2.35	

Figure 1-1 Flat Yield Curve, 10% level

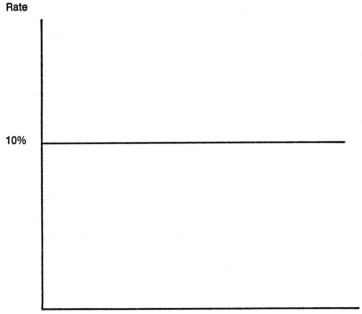

Security II declines in value while the market price of Security I remains unchanged. In fact, unless two portfolios' cash flows are identical in amount and timing, some twist in the yield curve is possible which will change the securities' values by different amounts, even if their BPVs and durations are identical.

Slope Point Value

The limitations imposed by the flat yield curve/parallel shift assumption of BPV and duration analysis can be overcome in part by the measurement of a *slope point value* (SPV) for securities. Assume that the yield curve is a linear function of time to maturity:

$$r_t = a + b \times t$$

where

r_t = the market's required return on a security paying a single cash flow at time t

a = the required return on overnight investments

b = a parameter describing the difference in rates corresponding to a given difference in time to maturity.

For instance, if a = .10 and b = .005, then an overnight investment will yield 10%; a one-year pure discount security will yield .10 + .005 = .105 or 10.5%, and so forth.

In the previous example, the yield curve started out flat at a level of 10%, meaning that

$$r_t = .10 + 0 \times t.$$

After the yield curve twisted, the curve was described by

$$r_t = .08 + .005 \times t.$$

When the yield curve is flat, we know that BPV describes what happens if the level of the curve, described by parameter a, shifts upward by .0001, for example, from

$$r_t = .10 + 0 \times t$$

to

$$r_t = .1001 + 0 \times t.$$

Slope point value describes what happens if the slope parameter b changes by .0001, for example, from

$$r_t = .10 + 0 \times t$$

to

$$r_t = .10 + .0001 \times t.$$

Using a combination of SPV and BPV, we can predict the effects of the yield curve shift in our original example with much greater accuracy than with BPV alone. For Security I, the slope point value is calculated as follows:

Yield Curve	Year (t)	r	Cashflow	Present Value	Total
$r = .10 + 0 \times t$	4	.10	$200.00	$136.60	
					$136.60
$r = .10 + .0001 \times t$	4	.1004	$200.00	$136.40	
					$136.40
				Slope Point Value:	$ .20

For Security II, SPV is

Yield Curve	Year (t)	r	Cashflow	Present Value	Total
$r = .10 + 0 \times t$	2	.10	$ 82.64	$68.30	
	6	.10	$121.00	$68.30	
					$136.60
$r = .10 + .0001 \times t$	2	.1002	$ 82.64	$68.72	
	6	.1006	$121.00	$68.08	
					$136.35
				Slope Point Value:	$ .25

In our original example, a changed from .10 to .08, or by 200 basis points, and b changed from 0 to .005, or by 50 slope points. Using both BPV and SPV, the predicted change in the price of Security I becomes

$$-200 \times \$.05 + 50 \times \$.20 = \$0.00,$$

exactly as observed, while the predicted change in the price of Security II becomes

$$-200 \times \$.05 + 50 \times \$.25 = \$2.50,$$

which is very close to the observed change of $2.35. The small difference between the actual and predicted price changes occurs because both BPV and SPV are perfectly accurate predictors only of the effects of very small changes in yield curve level or slope. As the example suggests, however, BPV and SPV in practice are fairly robust over large changes in slope or level.

Slope point value is easy to apply to portfolios and balance sheets, as well as to individual securities. The SPV of a portfolio is equal to the sum of the SPVs of the portfolio's components. The SPV of a balance sheet equals the sum of all asset SPVs, minus the sum of all liability SPVs.

Slope point value, the way we have defined it so far, also suffers from its own set of limitations. If the yield curve is not a straight line, a linear function will not describe it, and SPV calculations based on the linear function will be less accurate. If the yield curve kinks or curls in the middle, even nonlinear variations on slope point value will fail to predict the effect on security values.

In many rate risk management situations, BPV can be used to predict the bulk of the effect of any likely change in the yield curve, and a judgmental approach to the control of curve twist risk will suffice. In other situations, however, SPV can markedly enhance a risk manager's understanding of the rate risk problem at hand.

From Theory to Practice: Useful Tools and Techniques

Calculating the BPVs of 60 coupons and summing them to get the BPV of a Treasury bond is a long, tedious job. Fortunately, it is possible to utilize functions commonly found on financial calculators to do the job quickly and easily.

These functions all revolve around the relationship expressed in Equation 1-10.

$$P = \frac{C_1}{(1 + r)^1} + \frac{C_2}{(1 + r)^2} + \cdots + \frac{C_N + M}{(1 + r)^N} \quad (1\text{-}10)$$

where

P = the present value or market price of a coupon security or series of cash flows

$C_1 \ldots C_N$ = the cash flows occurring at times 1 through N

M = the principal amount paid at maturity

r = a rate of return.

The first function to consider is the *present value* (PV) function. Given the size of the cash flows, their timing, and the required rate of return r, present value is simply the value of P which makes Equation 1-10 true.

The second function to consider is the *yield to maturity* (YTM) function. Knowing a security's cash flows and their timing, and setting P to the market value of the security, YTM is the value of r which makes Equation 1-10 true. YTM is calculated by repeated guessing, until a value is guessed which makes Equation 1-10 true to the desired degree of accuracy.

Closely related to YTM is the *internal rate of return* (IRR) calculation. IRR is the same as YTM, except that the cash flows $C_1 \ldots C_N$ may be different in size from one another.

Using PV and YTM to Calculate the BPV
of a Coupon Security

Using PV and YTM, it is fairly easy to trick a financial calculator into computing the basis point value of a coupon security. The procedure is as follows:

1. Calculate the security's YTM. Use this YTM as an estimate of the market's required rate of return.
2. Reduce the YTM calculated in step 1 by half a basis point. Calculate the PV of the security using this reduced YTM as r.
3. Raise the YTM calculated in step 1 by half a basis point. Recalculate the security's PV using this increased YTM as r.
4. Subtract the PV calculated in step 3 from the PV calculated in step 2. This is the approximate basis point value of the security.
5. To adjust the BPV to reflect a standard face value, say $1 million. To do so, multiply the BPV obtained in step 4 by

$$\frac{1,000,000}{\text{face value used in calculation}}$$

This standardized BPV is referred to as BPV per million.

This method assumes that the yield curve is flat, with the market rate equal to YTM for all maturities. This results in an overstatement of BPV when the yield curve is positively sloped and in an understatement of BPV when the yield curve is negatively sloped. The calculation also results in a semiannually compounded BPV since standard bond calculations are done on a semiannually compounded basis.

Fast Calculation of Approximate Duration

Given a BPV calculated using this procedure, the approximate duration of a coupon security can be backed out using Equation 1-9:

$$D = \frac{\text{BPV}}{P} \times \frac{1+r}{.0001}.$$

There is, however, no convenient shortcut to the calculation of SPV.

Conclusion

Rate risk is the nemesis of investors and issuers of fixed income securities. Duration, BPV, and SPV give us an understanding of rate risk in many situations, but not the means to neutralize it. A variety of tools are available to control rate risk, but they are complex and, therefore, must be used knowledgeably to be effective.

Chapter 2 describes the forces governing the behavior of one type of rate risk management tool—fixed income futures contracts. In coming to understand futures price behavior, you will master two concepts: the *pricing principle* and *arbitrage*, which are crucial to understanding swaps and options as well. In addition, you will learn how to use duration and BPV to measure the interest sensitivity of futures contracts, giving you a single set of tools for analyzing both cash-market securities and futures.

CHAPTER 2

The Nature and Behavior of Futures

Overview

Exposure to rate risk arises in many situations. An investor may have special expertise in selecting long-maturity investments but have a short-term investment time horizon. A borrower may need funds for a long period of time but lack the ability to issue long-term liabilities. Futures contracts offer a means of reducing rate risk in these and many other situations. In this chapter, the essential features of futures and the forces which govern their price behavior and rate sensitivity will be described.

Forward Securities

The idea of a *forward security* is the conceptual link between cash market securities, such as bills and notes, and financial futures. A forward security is bought or sold now, but is not paid for until some date in the future. The life of a cash market pure discount bill is graphed on a time line as in Figure 2-1:

Figure 2-1 Events in the Life of a Cash Bill

Time 0	1	2	3
Agreement made to buy bill at price X; price paid and bill delivered.	... Bill appreciates ...	Face value received by buyer at maturity.	

19

In contrast, the life of a forward bill is graphed as in Figure 2-2.

In the case of the cash bill, the purchase or sale agreement, payment, and delivery all occur at the same time. In the case of the forward bill, the purchase or sale agreement is made now, but payment, transfer of ownership, and the start of interest accrual to the buyer do not occur until a later date specified in the purchase or sale agreement.

Consider for a moment the advantages of being able to buy or sell forward securities:

- An investor, knowing that a sum of cash will be available to invest at some date in the future, could buy a forward security for the amount of cash he needs to invest. The investor would then be certain of the yield he would earn on the cash.

- Conversely, the investor may know it is necessary to liquidate securities at a date prior to their maturity. The investor could then sell those securities forward, knowing well in advance the price he would receive for them.

- A borrower, anticipating a need for funds at some future date, could sell or short a forward security at a price equal to the amount of borrowing required. Then, knowing in advance the cost of borrowing, the borrower could gauge in advance the profitability of the project to be funded.

- A speculator could buy or sell forward securities to exploit an anticipated change in rates without immediately having to invest capital in the debt markets.

Figure 2-2 Events in the Life of a Forward Bill

Time 0	1	2	3
Agreement made to buy bill for price X at time 1.	Price X paid, bill delivered	. . Bill appreciates . . .	Face value received by buyer at maturity.

- An observer could learn now what rates of return or costs of funds are obtainable in the future by observing the prevailing prices of forward securities.

In a perfect market, free of transaction costs, these advantages could be accrued using combinations of bought and sold cash securities. However, in the real world the required cash securities do not always exist, and transaction costs are not trivial. For these reasons forward securities can have an irreplaceable role to play in the financial marketplace.

A financial futures contract is simply a special kind of forward security: a standardized, enforceable contract, traded on a centralized, regulated exchange, to buy or sell a specific type and amount of debt security at a prearranged price on a specified future date.

Futures Contracts

In the 1970s, financial futures evolved from three predecessors: (1) futures markets for physical commodities, (2) futures on currencies, and (3) the forward market for Government National Mortgage Association (GNMA or Ginnie Mae) securities, a type of government agency security.

Farmers in the 1800s sought protection from wide fluctuations in crop prices by making agreements well before harvest to sell their crops at contractually stipulated prices. As this practice became widespread, exchanges were formed on which forward contracts for standardized amounts and grades of agricultural products were traded. These standardized contracts were known as *futures*. Later, contracts were developed for livestock, metals, and other physical commodities subject to large price fluctuations.

After fixed currency exchange rates were abandoned in 1972, exchange rate volatility led to the creation of the International Monetary Market (IMM), an exchange affiliated with the Chicago Mercantile Exchange and devoted to trading in futures on currencies.

At the same time, GNMA securities were being produced and sold in large numbers, giving impetus to the development of GNMA futures. GNMAs are created when mortgage bankers assemble a pool of mortgages and have them approved, and thus guaranteed, by the federal government. As rates became increasingly volatile in the 1970s, GNMA originators naturally sought to reduce risk by selling GNMAs forward, before the underlying mortgage pools were assembled. The forward market became so well developed that it appeared feasible to initiate a GNMA futures contract. In October, 1975 the Chicago Board of Trade did so; shortly, thereafter, various other exchanges created contracts on U.S. Treasury bills, notes, and bonds, certificates of deposit, and Eurodollar time deposits.

From time to time futures markets are blamed for increasing the price volatility of commodities. Legislative attempts to ban futures trading have been defeated in light of the overriding social benefits provided by futures: they permit risk to be transferred to those most willing to bear it, and they permit discovery of prices that market participants collectively believe are most likely to prevail in the future.

While legislative bans on futures have been defeated, regulations have been promulgated which inhibit fraud, collusion, and monopolism. Currently, the Commodities Futures Trading Commission (CFTC) regulates the form and activities of all exchanges on which futures contracts are traded. The National Futures Association is an industry self-regulatory body sanctioned by the CFTC, which acts as watchdog against abusive practices. Both the Chicago Mercantile Exchange and the Chicago Board of Trade maintain internal departments or member committees overseeing business conduct, floor conduct, arbitration of disputed trades, as well as trade investigation and audit to preclude fraud, collusion, or other misconduct.

Forwards versus Futures

Financial futures contracts are distinguished from forward securities by four features: standardization, centralization, cash flows, and liquidity.

Standardization. Forward contracts can be tailor-made agreements between two contracting parties, with the amount and grade of deliverable securities, location and method of delivery, and delivery date specified in the contract chosen solely for the convenience of the contracting parties. In contrast, futures contracts are by nature completely standardized as to deliverable securities, delivery procedure, and other features.

Centralization. Forward contracts specify a price agreed on in private by the two contracting parties. Forward contracts may be entered into at any time and in any location. No one stands between buyer and seller in a forward agreement. Futures contracts are created and dissolved in a completely centralized fashion. Buyers and sellers bid to buy and offer to sell futures by open outcry in a single marketplace—a trading pit in a futures exchange. The hours in which trading occurs are set by the exchange administration. At any moment, all buyers and sellers trade futures at the highest bid price or the lowest offered price. A futures position is established when buyer and seller agree, person-to-person, on a price and quantity. However, as soon as the trade is made, the exchange clearing corporation steps between buyer and seller, backing the transaction with the full faith and credit of the clearing corporation and its member firms.

Cash flows. Once a price is agreed on in a forward contract, the price remains the same until the delivery date of the contract, when that price is paid and the securities are transferred. No cash changes hands until the delivery date. In contrast, the price of a futures agreement changes from minute to minute in the trading pit. How, then, can a forward buying or selling price be captured using futures? The answer lies in an understanding of futures *margin*.

The buyer or seller of futures contracts is required to post a performance bond or *initial margin* set by the exchange for each futures contract in his position. This margin is posted in cash or short-term Treasury securities to the firm that clears the position holder's trades. At the end of each trading day, his position is marked to market and the cash value of any change in the price of the position is added to or removed from the position margin account.

One effect of the margin account and the flow of variation margin is to permit a futures position holder to capture an effective forward price, even though the prices of his futures contracts change continuously. The current price of a futures contract, plus or minus variation margin received or paid, must equal the price of the futures contract when the contract was initially bought or sold. A second effect of the margin mechanism is that, since literal delivery is unnecessary, securities can be cross-hedged, using futures contracts into which they cannot be delivered.

Liquidity. Standardization, centralization, and the margin mechanism all act to promote great liquidity in the futures markets. The fact that all futures contracts of a given type have identical specifications eliminates the need to negotiate terms. Standardization also makes it easy to unwind a trade once it has been established, simply by selling to offset an existing "long" position or by buying to offset an existing "short" position. Parties to a customized forward agreement cannot get into or out of an agreement so easily. Centralization allows the exchange to stand between buyer and seller, ensuring the integrity of the contract. This insurance function makes futures market participants relatively indifferent to each others' identity and hence more willing to trade. In forward agreements, contract integrity equals the integrity of the parties involved. Participation in forward agreements, therefore, is likely to be more selective. Variation margin compensates futures holders in cash before delivery for fluctuations in market levels. Thus it is unnecessary to hold a futures contract through delivery to accrue the benefits of holding a forward security. In fact, only 3 percent of all futures positions are ever held to delivery. The rest are simply offset after their purpose has been served. This reduces the transaction costs of using futures as compared to forward agreements.

A summary comparison of forward agreements and futures contracts is presented in Table 2-1.

Futures Price Behavior

Having looked at what futures are, we can now look at how they behave in relation to other securities at a given time and over time. Common sense tells us that competing merchants who wish to make sales will try to match each others' prices; consumers otherwise will buy only from the merchant who offers the lowest price. We expect that price differences will persist only if buyers lack information or if the competing merchants are in

Table 2-1 Forward Contracts vs. Futures

Characteristic	Forward Contracts	Futures
Standardization		
Type, amount of deliverable security	At discretion of contracting parties	Standardized grade, face value of securities to be delivered
Delivery date, delivery procedure	At convenience of parties	Standardized as to allowable days and hours, delivery procedure
Performance bond	Discretionary	Standard performance bond (margin) posted by all position holders
Substitutions, other discretionary choices	May vary from agreement to agreement	Discretion always goes to short (seller)
Centralization		
Pricing	Privately determined, unchanging over life of agreement	Determined by open outcry in a central marketplace.
Contract integrity	Equals integrity of parties involved	Exchange steps between buyer and seller, backs all trades with full faith and credit of clearing corporation and its members
Regulation	No formal ad hoc regulatory body	Commodity Futures Trading Commission regulates exchanges
Cashflows	at delivery only	Payments made or received for each day's price movement (variation margin)
Liquidity	Low; parties well known to each other to reduce default risk; delivery is usually intended	High; low default risk makes parties indifferent to each other's identity; delivery is rare since margin flows produce desired effect.

reality selling dissimilar goods. Analogous behavior in the financial markets enable us to define a pricing principle which should guide our expectations about futures price behavior:

Similar securities tend to earn similar rates of return.

To understand this pricing principle and the mechanisms which enforce it in the marketplace is to understand the behavior of financial futures.

Two securities are similar to the extent that both will produce the same cash flow pattern with the same degree of certainty. A security, in the sense used here, may be a single instrument or a bundle of them, say, a combination of cash bills and futures contracts. An investor interested only in the cash flows to be received will be indifferent when choosing between two securities which are extremely similar.

To illustrate, consider a $1 million face value, three-month pure discount government bill; a six-month bill; and a futures contract for delivery of a three-month bill three months hence. The combination of one type of cash bill and a futures position comprises a synthetic security which is quite similar to a position in the other type of bill. For instance, buying three-month bills and the futures is similar to owning six-month bills; conversely, buying six-month bills and selling futures is similar to owning three-month bills. These cases are depicted in Figures 2-3 and 2-4.

If the pricing principle holds true, the futures contract in the these examples should be priced so that the synthetic securities (the cash and futures combinations) have the same returns as the natural securities to which they are similar. Expressed in another way, the final value of a dollar invested in either a natural security or its synthetic equivalent should be the same. Thus, in the case of the similar securities of Figure 2-3.

$$\$1 \times (1 + r_{3mo})^{.25} \times (1 + r_{fut})^{.25} = \$1 \times (1 + r_{6mo})^{.5}$$

where
r_{3mo} = annualized rate on three-month cash bill
r_{fut} = annualized forward rate on bill futures
r_{6mo} = annualized rate on six-month cash bill.

Figure 2-3 Similar Six-Month Securities

A. Buy three-month bills, buy futures

0	3 months	6 months
Buy 3-month bills; buy futures	bills mature; use proceeds to take delivery on futures	Receive face value of delivered bills

B. Buy and hold six-month bills

0	3 months	6 months
Buy six-month bills		Receive face value of bills

Figure 2-4 Similar Three-Month Securities

A. Buy six-month bills, sell futures

0	3 months	6 months
Buy 6-month bills; sell futures	deliver cash bills into futures contracts receive futures invoice price	

B. Buy and hold three-month bills

0	3 months	6 months
Buy 3-month bills	Receive face value of bills	

Given the rates on the cash bills*, the rate on the futures must equal

$$r_{fut} = \left(\frac{(1 + r_{6mo})^{.5}}{(1 + r_{3mo})^{.25}} \right)^{(1/.25)} - 1$$

Then, if three-month bills yield 5% and six-month bills yield 10%, the futures must yield

---

*The bill here is a hypothetical pure discount security, the rate/price relationships of which are measured by the methods described in Chapter 1. Real Treasury bills and bill futures are priced using a discount method.

$$\left(\frac{1.10^{.5}}{1.05^{.25}}\right)^4 - 1 = .1524 \text{ or } 15.24\%$$

and have an invoice price of

$$\frac{\$1,000,000}{1.1524^{.25}} = \$965,159.72.$$

Arbitrage

That similar securities earn similar rates of return is no mere assertion. There is a mechanism at work in the marketplace which enforces this pricing principle with unfailing vigor. That mechanism is called *arbitrage*. Arbitrage is the art of earning a profit while making no investment and assuming no market risk. Opportunities for arbitrage arise whenever the pricing principle is significantly violated. Execution of arbitrages tends to push prices back into the relationships predicted by the pricing principle.

Most pure arbitrage in the financial futures markets requires the ability to borrow or lend against securities posted as collateral and to buy or short-sell futures and cash securities. The taking or making of collateralized loans in the government securities market is accomplished via *repurchase agreements* and *reverse repurchase agreements.* In a repurchase agreement or repo, a borrower obtains funds by selling a government security and at the same time agrees to buy back or repurchase the security on a later date at a slightly higher price. The form of the arrangement is an agreement to sell and an agreement to buy at a later date. The economic effect is that a borrower has obtained funds for a period of time by posting a security as collateral. On a known future date, principal and interest will be paid, and the collateral returned. A reverse repurchase agreement (or reverse repo) is the same transaction from the perspective of the lender. The lender buys a government security and agrees to sell it back on a later date at a slightly higher price.

The nature of a purchase or sale of futures, or of a purchase of cash securities, is readily understood. A short-sale of cash securities requires more explanation. A short-seller is someone who borrows a security and then sells it, hoping to be able to buy it back at a later date for a lower price. A short-sale of government securities usually is part of a reverse repo. A short-seller first enters into a reverse repo agreement and receives a security that will have to be returned on a known future date. This security is then sold to effect a short-sale.

Typically, the repo rate is significantly higher than the reverse repo rate for a given security. This reflects in part a bid-asked spread typical of any market. It also incorporates a short-sale fee imposed on those wishing to reverse repo. A rational investor would want to charge a fee to someone wishing to borrow a security; the repo market does the same by offering a lower rate of return to lenders, reflecting the potential to short-sell via a reverse repo agreement.

The Cash and Carry Arbitrage

The simplest type of arbitrage is called the *cash and carry*. It entails the financed purchase of a security and delivery of the security into a short futures contract. The gain from buying the cash security at one price and selling it at the futures price more than offsets the cost of financing the security in the repo market, that is, the cost of carry. To illustrate, consider the government bills described earlier and a futures contract. The initial prices of the bills and futures are shown in Table 2-2.

A cash and carry in these securities would involve purchasing the six-month bill, financing it for three months at the three-month term repo rate, and selling the relatively overpriced futures contract. A profit is realized on delivery of the bill into the futures contract, as seen in Table 2-3.

Because there is no cash outlay, the arbitrager can demand six-month bills and repo rate loans and can supply futures, until the market rates on six-month bills, repo loans, and futures move enough to make further arbitrage unprofitable.

Table 2-2 Cash and Carry Example

Security	Price	Yield
3-month cash bill	$987,876	5%
6-month cash bill	953,463	10
Bill futures contract	976,454	10
Repo rate, 3-month bill	½% over 3-month bill rate	

Table 2-3 Cash and Carry Profit Analysis

Time	Event	Cash flows
Now	Buy 6 month bill	$−953,463
	Finance in repo market	953,463
	Sell futures	0
	New investment/return	0
In three months	Deliver bill into futures	976,454
	Repay repo principal and interest*	−966,573
	Net investment/return	$ 9,881

*Straight-line, 360-day rate for repos; all others compounded annually.

Reverse Cash and Carry Arbitrage

Were the futures in Table 2-3 priced to yield 25% rather than 10%, a second type of arbitrage would be possible; the *reverse cash and carry*. The invoice price on a futures at 25% is $945,742. To execute a reverse cash and carry, an arbitrager would enter into a reverse repo agreement to obtain the bill to be delivered into the futures contract. He would then sell the bill and buy the futures contract. On the futures delivery date, he would take delivery of the bill, return it to the other side of the reverse repo, and receive repo principal and interest. Table 2-4 details the transactions and resultant profits from this reverse cash and carry.

Table 2-4 Reverse Cash and Carry Profit Analysis

Time	Event	Cash flows
Now	Sell 6 month bill	$ 953,463
	Lend proceeds of short sale via reverse repo	−953,463
	Buy futures	0
	Net investment/return	0
In three months	Take delivery on futures	−945,742
	Receive repo principal and interest*	965,381
	Net investment/return	$ 19,639

*Assumes 5% repo rate.

As in the cash and carry, an arbitrager doing the reverse cash and carry in theory can supply deliverable cash securities and repo funds and can demand futures contracts, until prices move enough to render further trading profitless. Some complications arise in practice because discretion concerning delivery time and allowable substitutions is always given to the seller of futures, while the arbitrager in a reverse cash and carry is long futures. Because what is delivered and when delivery occurs can be uncertain, reverse cash and carry is not as tight a constraint on cash/futures relationships as the cash and carry.

Quasi-Arbitrage

Quasi-arbitrage is identical to pure arbitrage in all respects except that the cash security involved, rather than being purchased and financed or short sold, is purchased using the trader's own capital, is already owned, or is sold out of existing inventory. The motive for quasi-arbitrage is not to profit with no investment or risk, but to create an alternative to existing investments which yields higher returns with no increase in investment or risk.

Because the cash securities involved in quasi-arbitrage are not financed, the effect of the bid-asked spread in the repo market is not a factor in determining the profitability of the trade. Thus quasi-arbitrage can be done even when arbitrage cannot. Because it requires investor capital, however, quasi-arbitrage is not as strong a force in the market as pure arbitrage.

To illustrate quasi-arbitrage, consider the three- and six-month bills and the bill futures used in the reverse cash and carry example. Suppose these securities were priced as shown in Table 2-5.

As shown in Table 2-6, a pure reverse cash and carry is not

Table 2-5 Quasi-Arbitrage Example

Security	Price	Yield
3-month cash bill	$987,876	5.00%
6-month cash bill	953,463	10.00
Bill futures contract	964,095	15.75
Rate on 3-month reverse repo		4.00

Table 2-6 Profit Analysis: Reverse Cash and Carry vs. Quasi-Arbitrage

Reverse Cash and Carry, Pure Arbitrage

Time	Event	Cash flows
Now	Sell six-month bill	$-953,463
	Lend proceeds of short sale via reverse repo	953,463
	Buy futures	0
	Net investment/return	0
In three months	Take delivery on futures	-964,095
	Receive repo principal and interest	962,998
	Net investment/return	$- 1,097

Quasi-Arbitrage Reverse Cash and Carry

Yield to owing three-month bill and futures:

$$(1.05^{.25} \times 1.1575^{.25})^{(1/.5)} - 1 = .1024 \text{ or } 10.24\%$$

Increase in yield compared to holding six-month bills: .24%

profitable with these relationships. However, the owner of six-month bills could profit by selling them and buying three-month bills and futures.

Measures of Arbitrage Profit Potential

There are many ways to gauge the profitability of potential arbitrage opportunities. Perhaps the most straightforward is to calculate arbitrage profit, as shown in Equation 2-1:

$$AP = FP - [CP \times (1 + r \times n/360)] \qquad (2\text{-}1)$$

where

AP = arbitrage profit, in dollars

FP = futures invoice price

CP = deliverable cash security price

r = term repo rate to delivery (straight line, 360-day basis)

n = number of days from initiating the arbitrage until delivery.

If the repo rate is used for *r* in this formula, cash and carry is profitable whenever *AP* is positive. If the reverse repo rate is used for *r*, reverse cash and carry is profitable whenever *AP* is negative. Notice that whenever there is a difference between the repo and reverse repo rates, there is a range of futures prices over which no arbitrage is profitable.

A second measure of arbitrage profit potential is the break-even repo rate—the maximum repo rate an arbitrager can afford to pay without losing money in a cash and carry, or the minimum reverse repo rate the arbitrager can afford to receive to avoid loss in a reverse cash and carry. The *break-even repo rate* (BERR) is calculated using Equation 2-2:

$$BERR = \frac{FP - CP}{CP} \times \frac{360}{n} \qquad (2\text{-}2)$$

where

BERR = the break-even repo rate in a cash and carry.

Notice that as long as the actual repo rate is higher than *BERR* or the actual reverse repo rate is lower than *BERR*, profitable arbitrage is precluded.

A third measure of arbitrage profit potential is the fair futures price—the futures price which would permit no profitable arbitrage. Fair futures price is calculated using Equation 2-3:

$$FFP = CP \times [1 + (r \times n/360)] \qquad (2\text{-}3)$$

where

FFP = fair futures price.

All of these measures assume that there is no uncertainty about which security will be delivered into the futures contract and that the exact delivery date can be predicted in advance. Violations in these assumptions can distort arbitrage relationships in practice.

These measures are in generic form, i.e., they can be used to evaluate any futures contract, once all prices are expressed in dollars and cents. Modified *BERR* formulas will be provided in Chapter 3 to allow easier calculation when prices are quoted on an index rather than in dollars. The concept behind the calculations is the same.

Basis

Arbitrage relationships imply a definite relationship between deliverable cash security prices and futures prices, given the level of term repo rates. The possibility of cash and carry arbitrage places a limit on how high futures prices can rise relative to cash prices; the possibility of reverse cash and carry places a limit on how low futures prices can sink relative to cash prices. *Basis* is the term used to describe the relationship between a deliverable cash security price and the corresponding futures price.

"Basis" is used very imprecisely in the futures industry. For example, "*bill basis*" is often used to describe the relationship between the current 90-day bill and a bill futures contract for delivery in six months, even though the cash bill will have matured by the delivery date. Another common use is to describe the relationship between cash and futures of two different security types; for example, a bill futures and a Treasury note. Very often, basis is applied to the relationship between a deliverable cash security and the corresponding futures, but it is expressed in terms of a rate-based index or some other convention which obscures the underlying arbitrage relationship.

In a narrower definition, *basis* is the difference between the futures invoice price and the price of the deliverable cash security, expressed in dollars, or

$$Basis = FP - CP. \qquad (2\text{-}4)$$

Combining Equations 2-3 and 2-4, it becomes clear that

$$Basis = FP - CP = CP \times r \times n/360. \qquad (2\text{-}5)$$

$CP \times r \times n/360$ may be interpreted as the total interest expense incurred to finance—or carry—a cash security until it is delivered into a futures contract. This total interest expense is also called the *cost of carry* or simply *carry*. Thus, we can say that *basis equals carry*. While complications arise because of multiple deliverable securities and delivery dates, the notion that basis equals carry can be used to explain the largest part of cash/futures relationships.

Basis Behavior Over Time

Many futures market participants use strategies which begin and end within a day or two. For these users, it is sufficient to have only a snapshot of the basis at the time a trade is implemented. Many other futures users select strategies which require a cash-futures position which will be left in place for weeks or even months. These longer-term strategies can be seriously affected by changes in the basis over time. Fortunately, it is possible to predict the behavior of the basis over time using the concept of carry, and an understanding of the expected behavior of the yield curve over time (see Appendix 1).

The easiest case to consider is that of a nine-month pure discount bill, deliverable into a futures contract six-months hence, when the straight-line or simple rate yield curve is flat. The basis between the cash bill and the futures over time is depicted in Figure 2-5.

In a flat yield curve environment, the one-day forward rates are all the same, equal to the term rate at any point on the curve. If the expectations built into this yield curve are realized, the cash bill should appreciate in market value at the same rate (by the same amount) each day, until it is worth its maturity value after nine months. The price line in Figure 2-5, therefore, is a straight line with a slope equal to the market rate.

If the expectations built into this yield curve are realized, the futures price stays constant over time. Forward rates are equal to term rates, so no change in the shape or level of the yield curve is anticipated by the market. The term *repo rate* is the same as the yield on the cash bill; each day the remaining cost of carry on the bill diminishes by the amount that the price of the cash bill increases. Since the fair futures price equals the cash price plus carry, the futures price remains unchanged.

Consider next the case of a one-time parallel upward shift in the yield curve after three months, as depicted in Figure 2-6.

In this case, the cash bill experiences a one-time drop in market value after three months, and thereafter appreciates at the new, higher market rate until its market value reaches its maturity value after nine months. After the rise in rates, an arbi-

Figure 2-5 Basis Over Time: Flat, Constant Yield Curve Case

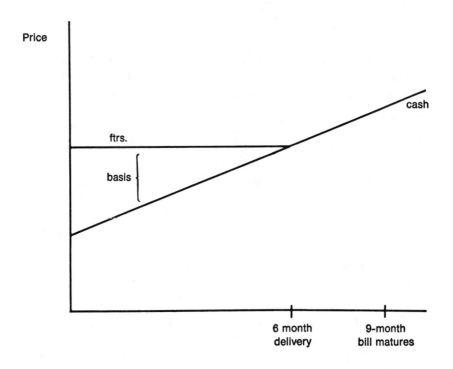

trager can borrow less to finance the bill; however, a higher repo rate must be paid. The net effect is that the futures contract declines in price by a smaller amount than the bill, and, thereafter, does not change in price if market expectations are realized.

More complicated still is the case of a positively sloped yield curve. In this case, the one-day forward rates are rising over time. If market expectations are realized, the cash bill will appreciate by a small amount each day during the first few months, and more rapidly during the last months of its life. Its price appreciation path is, therefore, a curved line. Nonetheless, the futures price line is straight and flat. As time passes, the expected term repo rate to delivery will increase and the price of the cash bill will increase by some amount. These changes will be offset exact-

Figure 2-6 Basis Over Time: Flat Curve, Parallel Shift

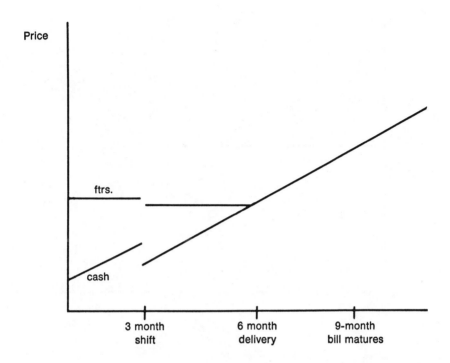

Price

ftrs.

cash

3 month shift   6 month delivery   9-month bill matures

ly by the reduction in the number of days to delivery, leaving the sum of cash price and carry unchanged. This case is shown in Figure 2-7.

Consider, next, the case of a change in the slope of the field curve, from flat to positively sloped. In particular, assume a pivot in the yield curve around the nine month maturity point, so that the nine-month term rate is unchanged, while rates for terms less than nine months are lower than before. The behavior of basis in this case is shown in Figure 2-8.

The term rate on the cash bill is unchanged, so its price does not change on the day the curve twists. However, from that point on, the bill's price will appreciate more slowly than before, and

Figure 2-7 Basis Over Time: Positively Sloped Yield Curve

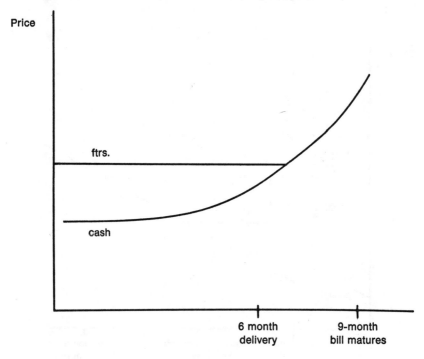

then at an accelerating rate as the bill approaches maturity. At the time of the pivot, the repo rate, and hence carry, will decline. The futures price will fall with the sum of cash price and carry. Thereafter, the basis will behave as in Figure 2-7. If the curve became negatively sloped (or inverted) rather than positively sloped, the basis would behave as shown in Figure 2-9.

The pricing principle implies that by buying a nine-month bill and delivering it into a futures contract in six months, we create a synthetic six-month security which earns a six-month term rate. This result is implicit in Figure 2-7. When the yield curve is positive, the nine-month term rate is higher than the six-month term rate. By delivering the cash bill into the futures, the bill is given up for the part of its life during which it earns the

Figure 2-8 Basis Over Time: Yield Curve Pivots Upward

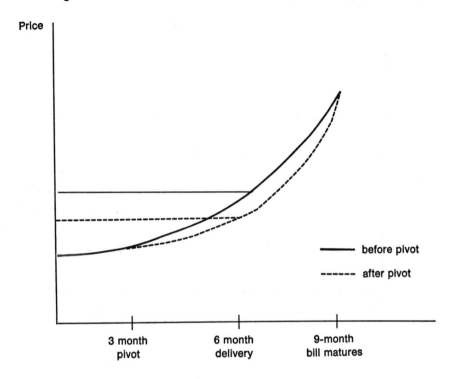

highest rate of return. The result is to reduce the experienced rate of return to a six month rate. If the yield curve is negatively sloped, delivery occurs when the bill is about to experience the lowest rate of return, raising the experienced rate of return to the six month term rate.

Interestingly, it is not necessary that market expectations be realized for the pricing principle to prevail. Consider the case of a positive yield curve environment in which the cash bill none-theless experiences a constant rate of return over its life, as depic-ted in Figure 3-10. In this case, the futures price will actually rise over time, resulting in a loss which will reduce the total rate of return to the six-month term rate.

Figure 2-9 Basis Over Time: Yield Curve Inverts

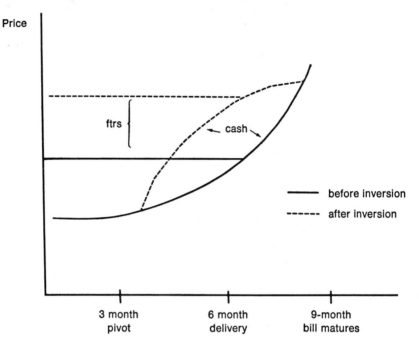

The Interest Sensitivity of Financial Futures

A final link between cash and futures is a method of quantifying the interest sensitivity of a futures contract. The most obvious method to use in light of the previous discussion is to see how arbitrage moves futures prices when overall interest rates move by one basis point.

Consider a perfect world with no transaction costs, in which there is one futures contract calling for delivery in six months of a three-month bill, one nine-month bill, and a repo market. The yield curve is flat. The futures invoice price is $975,000 and the deliverable bill's price is $926,857.33. By the rate equation and by our flat yield curve assumption, the yield on the deliverable bill, the implied forward rate on the futures, and the repo rate for any term all equal .10658.

Figure 2-10 Basis Over Time: Positively Sloped Yield Curve
Constant Yield Assumedd for Cash Bill

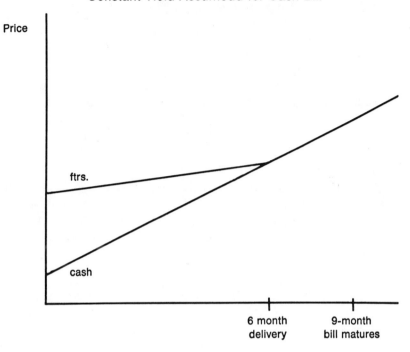

Price

ftrs.

cash

6 month
delivery

9-month
bill matures

   Arbitrage suggests that the futures price must equal the cash price plus carry. If the market rate were half a basis point lower, the futures price would be

$$\text{New Cash Price} \times (1 + r - .00005)^{(n/360)}$$

$$\frac{\$1,000,000}{1.10653^{.75}} \times 1.10653^{.5} = \$975,010.30$$

   If the market rate were a half basis point higher than it is, the futures price would be

$$\frac{\$1,000,000}{1.10663^{.75}} \times 1.10663^{.5} = \$974,988.27$$

The difference between these two arbitrage-created prices is

$$\$975,010.30 - \$974,988.27 = \$22.03.$$

The relationships in this arbitrage analysis of rate sensitivity boil down to a simpler relationship:

The BPV of a futures contract equals the BPV of the deliverable cash security, as it will appear on the delivery date.

This rule is exactly true when the yield curve is flat, and is a close approximation of the truth in markets characterized by all but the most extremely sloped yield curves.

In this example, the deliverable bill on the delivery date will have an effective price equal to the futures invoice price, $975,000, a rate equal to 10.658%, a one million dollar face value, and a quarter year to maturity. Its BPV, as for any cash security with like characteristics, is

$$\frac{\$1,000,000}{1.10653^{.25}} - \frac{\$1,000,000}{1.10663^{.25}} = \$22.03.$$

A corollary to the rule highlighted earlier is that:

The duration of a futures contract equals the duration of the deliverable security, as it will appear on the delivery date.

Effects of the Timing of Variation Margin Cash flows

A peculiarity of futures is that they result in cash flows today which equal the undiscounted change in an invoice price which will be paid at some time in the future. It is this feature which allows us to hedge today's market value of a security by simple BPV-matching against a futures contract which reflects the price of a forward security.

However, if the item being hedged is a price or cash flow to be paid far in the future, simple BPV matching will result in overhedging by ignoring the fact that positive variation margin can be invested and negative variation margin must be financed. An obvious case where the timing of variation margin can be important is in cash and carry trades, in which the futures position in effect hedges the future sale price for a bond. To correct for cash flow timing, the futures position must be reduced by a factor of

$$1/(1 + r_T)^T$$

where

T = the time until delivery of the security being carried.

r_T = the market investment rate for term T.

A cash and carry in bills adjusted for variation margin timing would involve the following securities:

Buy X million dollars in maturity value of deliverable bills

Sell $\dfrac{X}{(1 + r)^T}$ bill futures.

As T diminishes, the futures position is gradually increased.

Note that T is determined not by the time to delivery of the futures contracts being used but by the time until the occurrence of the event being hedged. Thus no adjustment is necessary when hedging the current value of a cash security, since the event being hedged is an immediate change in price.

Most practitioners ignore the effects of margin cash flow timing when designing futures positions. Nonetheless, when establishing a very large position or one which hedges an event occurring in the distant future, you should consider making an adjustment for margin cash flow timing effects.

Conclusion

The pricing principle and arbitrage are at the core of futures price behavior. They enforce a predictable relationship between futures prices and the prices of cash fixed-income securities, enabling us to extend duration and BPV analysis from cash securities to futures. Understanding arbitrage and the pricing principle also enables a rate risk manager to develop realistic expectations of hedge performance, and to distinguish valid trading strategies from the financial equivalent of perpetual motion machines.

The next step is to carry the clean and simple concepts of Chapter 2 into the quirky, cluttered real world. Chapter 3 describes the practical details of futures contract design and use and offers guidelines for relating the arbitrage and pricing principle concepts to the real-world futures contracts you are likely to use in day-to-day rate risk management.

CHAPTER 3

Analyzing Futures Contracts

Futures contract specifications have a direct impact on futures arbitrage relationships and, therefore, on futures behavior. Most contract specifications arose from historical accident rather than grand vision and occasionally obscure underlying theoretical relationships in the market. Learning to work with—and around—the contractual conventions of financial futures is prerequisite to their effective use.

Simple lists of various contract specifications are readily available; however, it is hard to find a systematic way to assess the impact of contract specifications on prices. To remedy this, Chapter 3 is divided into two parts. Part I offers a heuristic approach to evaluating contract specifications. Part II applies this approach to specific, currently traded contracts.

I. How to Assess Contract Specifications

A futures contract generally will specify the following:

1. A system for pricing the contracts, and for translating contract prices into an invoice price for the deliverable security.
2. A precise description of the deliverable security, including:
   a. Allowable issuers.
   b. Type of security.
   c. Allowable original maturity.
   d. Allowable time from delivery to maturity.
   e. Coupon, if applicable.

  f. Amount deliverable—generally in terms of *dollars of par value.*

3. A description of substitutions that can be made for the nominally deliverable security described earlier and of any adjustments to the invoice price (or face value) that must be made if a substitute security is delivered.
4. A list of times during which the contract may be traded.
5. A list of delivery months.
6. A rule determining the day or days during the delivery month on which delivery may be made.
7. Rules governing the delivery procedure, including:
    a. When the contract seller gives notice of intent to deliver.
    b. When the seller tenders securities for delivery, and in what form.
    c. When and how the contract buyer makes payment.
8. Limits on the number of contracts which may be accumulated by one party, and rules governing the conditions under which such limits may be waived.
9. Limits on the magnitude of price fluctuations that can occur in any one day, and provisions to expand those limits in especially volatile markets.
10. Procedures to match longs and shorts for delivery, to process payments, remedy nonperformance, and so on.

A futures market participant should ask seven questions about a given contract:

1. What does the contract price mean and how does it translate into the cost of the deliverable security?
2. How can prices of one type of futures contract be compared to the prices of other types of futures contracts?
3. How many different securities are deliverable, and how many potential arbitrage opportunities do they represent?
4. What is the effect of invoice price adjustments for substitute deliverable securities?
5. How is the cheapest deliverable security determined, and how does this affect contract price?

6. Do quirks and characteristics of the delivery process affect or create arbitrage situations?

7. Given the answers to these questions, what change in future invoice price will result from a given change in market rates? What variation margin flows will result?

Pricing Systems

Financial futures contracts are priced according to three systems: percent of par, add-on index, and discount index. These systems are not used for their conceptual elegance, but to meet three criteria: to match pricing practices in the market for the deliverable cash securities; to keep prices within a convenient range; and to keep constant the dollar value of a one unit price change.

Percent of Par

Percent of par, the simplest pricing system, is used to price the Treasury bond, Treasury note, GNMA, and municipal bond index futures contracts. The percent of par price of a futures contract expresses as a percent of face value the invoice price paid to take delivery of the nominally deliverable security, net of coupon accrual.

$$\text{Dollar Price} = \text{face value} \times \frac{\text{\% of Par Price}}{100} + \text{Coupon Accrual.}$$

$$(3\text{-}1)$$

For example, if a $100,000 face value 8% coupon Treasury bond were delivered into a contract priced at 89-00, the invoice price paid for the bond by the long position holder would be .89 × $100,000 or $89,000, plus coupon accrual. The effective yield to maturity of the delivered bond can be inferred from this invoice price.

Futures contract prices generally are based on some nominally deliverable cash security with a particular coupon (generally 8%). If a security with a nonnominal coupon is delivered into the futures contract, the futures price is multiplied by a conversion factor to arrive at the dollar futures invoice price. The conversion factors for various contracts will be discussed in detail in Part II of this chapter.

Coupon accrual is compensation paid the seller of a bond for having held the bond for a fraction of the time between coupon payments. Coupon accrual is never included in a quoted percent of par price, but it is always paid when a bond changes hands. On government bonds, accrued coupon income as a percent of face value is calculated as follows:

$$AI = .5 \times C \times \frac{DP}{TD} \qquad (3\text{-}2)$$

where

AI = accrued coupon income

C = annual coupon payment

DP = days passed since last coupon payment

TD = total days between last and next coupon payment.

By convention, fractions of a percent of par are quoted in 32nds, rather than in decimal form. Thus, a percent of par price of 89-16 equals 89 16/32 or 89.5 percent of par. To convert to decimal expression from 32nds, simply divide the fractional portion of the price by 32. To convert to 32nds from decimal, multiply the decimal portion by 32.

In futures contracts, 1/32nd is the minimum price fluctuation allowed. In the cash market, notes and bonds can trade in increments as small as 1/64th or even 1/128th. Some clumsy conventions have evolved for quoting these smaller increments; a plus (+) is added to the next lower 32nd price to denote plus 1/64th, and a 1 or a 3 is appended to the number of 32nds to denote plus 1/128th or plus 3/128ths, respectively. Other conventions are used by certain quotation systems.

Add-On Index

The *add-on index* pricing system is used to price Eurodollar futures traded on the Chicago Mercantile Exchange. As the name suggests, the add-on index is not a price itself but an index, equal to 100 minus the add-on rate expressed as a percent. Eurodollar time deposits and other short-term bank securities are typically traded on the basis of their add-on rates rather than their prices.

The add-on rate is similar to a straight-line, 360-day rate.

The term *add-on* is used because banks typically issue CDs or Eurodollar time deposits at par value and then add-on interest accrual to the maturity value of the instrument. The add-on rate is calculated as follows:

$$r_a = (M/I - 1) \times 360/n \qquad (3\text{-}3)$$

where

r_a = stated add-on rate, fixed at origination

M = the maturity value of the add-on instrument (principal plus all interest accrued from origination to maturity)

I = the initial investment (or face value) of the instrument.

n = the number of days remaining in the life of the instrument.

Setting n to the number of days from origination to final maturity, the maturity value of an add-on instrument is

$$M = I \times (I + r_a \times n/360). \qquad (3\text{-}4)$$

It is occasionally useful to calculate the dollar price of an add-on security when the current market rate is different from the original or stated rate of the security. To do so, calculate the maturity value of the security, M, and recalculate its present value, I', using the current market add-on rate, r_a' and the days remaining to maturity, n'.

$$I' = \frac{M}{1 + r_a' \times n'/360},$$

or

$$I' = I\frac{360 + r_a \times n}{360 + r_a' \times n'} \qquad (3\text{-}5)$$

where

I' = the present dollar price of the add-on security

r_a' = the present market add-on rate

n' = the days remaining in the life of the add-on security

Discount Index

The third pricing system, currently used for the Treasury bill contract, is the *discount index,* equal to 100 minus the discount.

The discount is calculated assuming a 360-day year. The denominator of the discount equation is the face value, not the market price of the discount security:

$$d = (F - P)/F \times 360/n \qquad (3\text{-}6)$$

where

d = Discount in decimal form

F = Face value of the discount security

P = Market price

n = Actual number of days from settlement to maturity.

Conversely, the market price of a discount security, given F and n, is

$$P = F \times [1 - d \times n/360]. \qquad (3\text{-}7)$$

Equation 3-7 is also used to calculate the futures invoice price. The discount is often referred to as the discount rate and is erroneously assumed to be a bona-fide rate of interest. It is not; it is an annualized percentage deduction (or discount) from par value, which can be used as an index to calculate the market price of a discount security. The difference between rate of return and the discount over a wide range of values is shown in Figure 3-1. It is clear that at any given level, the discount will change a little less than the rate.

Conversion Between Pricing Systems

It is often useful to compare the prices of two futures contracts quoted under different pricing systems. To make an undistorted comparison in this situation we must be able to convert from one pricing system to another. Generally, it is easiest to convert prices to rates and then compare the rates.

To convert from a discount to an add-on rate:

$$r_a = \frac{360}{n} \times \left(\frac{1}{1 - d \times n/360} - 1 \right). \qquad (3\text{-}8)$$

To convert from a discount to a *bond equivalent yield* (straight-line, 365-day rate):

$$BEY = \frac{d \times 365/360}{1 - d \times n/360}. \qquad (3\text{-}9)$$

Figure 3-1 The Difference Between Rate of Return and Discount
Over a Wide Range of Values

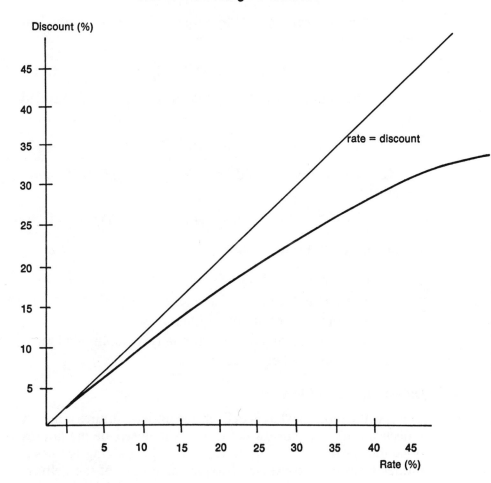

To convert from a discount to an annually compounded
rate:

$$r = \left(\frac{1}{1 - d \times n/360}\right)^{(365/n)} - 1. \qquad (3\text{-}10)$$

To convert from a discount to a semiannually compounded rate:

$$r = 2 \times \left[\left(\frac{1}{1 - d \times n/360} \right)^{[1/(2 \times n)]} - 1 \right]. \qquad (3\text{-}11)$$

To convert from an add-on rate to a bond equivalent yield:

$$BEY = r_a \times 365/360. \qquad (3\text{-}12)$$

To convert from an add-on rate to an annually compounded rate:

$$r = (1 + r_a \times n/360)^{(365/n)} - 1; \qquad (3\text{-}13)$$

To convert from an add-on rate to a semiannually compounded rate:

$$r = 2 \times [(1 + r_a \times n/360)^{[365/(2 \times n)]} - 1]. \qquad (3\text{-}14)$$

In equations 3-8 through 3-14,

r_a = the add-on rate
d = the discount
n = the days remaining to maturity
r = the annually (or semiannually) compounded rate
BEY = the bond equivalent yield.

Deliverable Securities

The specification of what is deliverable under a futures contract reflects a trade-off. Narrow definition will closely tie the futures price to a positively identified cash security, making the cash-futures basis easy to predict. Broader definition of the deliverable security will result in a larger potential supply of deliverable cash securities, heading off squeezes or the establishment of monopoly positions. In any case, specification of the deliverable cash security has more impact than any other contract feature on the number and nature of arbitrage possibilities.

Any time the specifications of what is deliverable allow more than one type of security to be delivered, the following will apply:

• There are more sources of supply to be monitored.

- There are more chances for arbitrage opportunities to arise and more data an arbitrager must monitor.
- The cash security most likely to be delivered may change over time, or may be indeterminable. If the list of allowable issues changes over time, cash and carry arbitrage may be made difficult.
- Any arbitrage that involves taking delivery on a long futures position is complicated since the long position holder has no control over what is delivered to him—and what is delivered may not meet the requirements of the arbitrage.

The specified original maturity of the deliverable cash security may control how many contract delivery dates in the future are subject to arbitrage relationships. For example, the U.S. Treasury bill contract at one time specified that the deliverable bill could have a maximum original time to maturity of less than one year. Original issue year bills could not be delivered, and no nine-month bills were issued by the Treasury. This meant that, in general, contracts only for the next one or two delivery months were subject to arbitrage.

Later, the contract was changed to allow delivery of original issue year bills, and contracts for the nearest three delivery months became subject to arbitrage. Conversely, arbitrage is possible on all contracts traded in Treasury bonds, which can be of any original maturity but must have 15 years or more from delivery to maturity.

Adjustments for Substitutions

Substitutions for the nominally deliverable cash securities generally entail an adjustment to the delivery price. In the case of futures on T-bills, the adjustment for substitutions consists simply of setting n to 91 or 92 in the appropriate invoice price calculation formula.

In the case of futures on coupon-bearing securities, a more substantial adjustment is made by multiplying the futures price by a conversion factor in arriving at an invoice price. The conversion factor addresses an obvious problem: If the futures invoice price were the same for any coupon security delivered into a futures contract, then all deliverers would strive to deliver a security with the lowest coupon possible. The relevant supply of deliverable securities would be shrunk, and arbitrage relationships would revolve around cash securities with atypical characteristics.

The goal of the conversion factor adjustment, then, is to make securities of all different coupons more or less equally desirable to deliver, by resulting in a higher invoice price for delivery of securities with higher coupons. The means by which the conversion factor is calculated are simple in concept: Determine the multiple of par value at which a deliverable security would be priced to yield 8% from delivery to the earlier of call or maturity. That multiple of par is the conversion factor. The factor will be greater than one for securities with coupons over 8% and less than one for securities with coupons less than 8%.

Some quirks in actual practice complicate conversion factor calculations. To facilitate the publishing of factor tables, official conversion factors are calculated using time from delivery to the earlier of call or maturity, rounded down to the nearest quarter year for T-bonds and ten-year T-note futures, and to the nearest month for five-year T-note futures. The resulting factors are rounded to four decimal places.

Adjustments for substitutions can have important effects on what is most likely to be delivered into a given futures contract and when delivery is most likely to occur. This, in turn, can affect futures price behavior.

One adjustment for substitutions is never made:

Marking to market and daily cash settlement are always computed on the basis of the nominally deliverable security.

This has important implications for futures contracts using conversion factors. When the note or bond futures price rises by one tick (1/32 percent of par), the futures invoice price rises by $31.25 times the conversion factor, but variation margin of only $31.25 is paid. To ensure that the variation margin compensates for invoice price changes, futures positions must be adjusted by the conversion factor.

Cheapness

The importance of *cheapness* in the futures market is demonstrated clearly by an extreme example. Suppose you have just sold at $300 a futures contract which calls for delivery of either an ounce of gold or one can of well-aged garbage. You intend to deliver. Which will you deliver, the gold or the garbage? Clearly, delivery of the gold might well result in a loss to you, while delivery of the garbage will result in a tidy profit. Delivery of anything but the cheapest of all deliverable items (here, the garbage) will reduce the profitability of delivery or increase its cost.

The same principle holds true for financial futures contracts: Short position holders, if rational, will try to deliver the cheapest allowable security into a futures contract. Long position holders who know this will not be willing to pay more for a futures contract than a price which reflects the value of the cheapest security likely to be delivered. Thus,

*Futures prices track most closely the price of the
expected cheapest deliverable security.*

It is simple to ascertain the cheapest deliverable security:

*The cheapest deliverable security is the one which earns
the greatest profit (least loss) in a cash and carry.*

To understand this result intuitively, consider three deliverable securities. Delivery in a cash and carry of the first would result in a $5 profit; of the second, a $25 loss; and of the third, a $50 profit. Clearly, arbitragers would buy the third security to the exclusion of the others as long as it was priced to give a profit greater than $5 in a cash and carry. Conversely, the arbitragers would avoid delivering the second security if at all possible.

Holders of a cash and carry position hold an option which can be of considerable value. Their profits are locked up in a pure cash and carry and cannot be diminished by changes in market prices. However, if a new security appears which is cheaper to deliver, arbitragers can increase their profits by selling their original security and replacing it with the new one. Because of the existence of this option, the arbitragers are willing to sell their futures contracts for a lower price, driving the break-even repo rates to lower levels than might otherwise be expected.

Conversion factor adjustments create significant biases in the determination of the cheapest-to-deliver security for futures on notes or bonds. If market yields exceed 8%, the conversion factor adjustment tends to make the longest duration security cheapest to deliver; conversely, if market yields are below 8%, securities with shorter duration are favored. These biases arise because conversion factors adjust perfectly for differences in coupon, but not differences in maturity, among various coupon securities.

Delivery Procedures

The days and times at which delivery is allowed can have a significant impact on futures prices. If delivery is allowed over a range of days, the day on which delivery is most likely to occur is the day on which total cash and carry arbitrage profits are likely to be maximized. This date is different for each contract and will be discussed in more detail in Part II of this chapter.

Quirks in the delivery process can also complicate basis relationships. The best known of these quirks is called the *wild card option*, which arises in note and bond futures. Short position holders in the note or bond contracts may give notice of intent to deliver on any day during roughly the first three weeks of the delivery month. Notice may be given until 8:00 p.m. Central time; notice given after the 2:00 p.m. close of the futures markets results in delivery at the closing futures price. The cash note or bond market stays open until 5:00 or 6:00 p.m.

Consider arbitragers in a cash and carry with $10 million in face value of cash bonds having a conversion factor of 1.5000. To ensure that the variation margin fully compensates for changes in the futures invoice price, arbitragers sell 150 bond futures against their cash position. Normally, arbitragers would hold their cash and carry until some date in the delivery month, then buy back 50 futures and deliver his cash bonds into the remaining hundred.

However, what can they do if bad news causes cash market prices to decline after the close of the futures markets during the delivery month? Arbitragers already have $10 million in cash bonds and cannot increase their arbitrage profits on them. However, instead of buying back their 50 extra contracts, they can buy $5 million more in cash bonds at the lower cash market price and deliver them into the extra contracts at the higher 2:00 p.m. futures price. In essence, arbitragers have a put option for a few hours each day during the first three weeks of the delivery month. This wild card option has value to the seller of futures, may affect basis relationships, and may bias arbitragers toward cash and carry trades using bonds with higher conversion factors when several bonds are equally cheap to deliver.

II. The Major Futures Contracts Today

Contract:	**Treasury Bill Futures**
Symbol:	TB
Exchange:	International Monetary Market (IMM), a division of the Chicago Mercantile Exchange.
Deliverable Security:	U.S. Treasury bills, original maturity not greater than one year, on the day of delivery having 92, 91, or 90 days left until maturity. The nominally deliverable maturity is 90 days. The most often delivered are 91-day bills.
Size of Delivery Unit:	$1,000,000 face value. All bills delivered under one contract must have the same maturity dates.
Pricing System:	Discount index for futures, discount for cash. Refer to Equations 3-6 and 3-7.
Invoice Price Calculation:	Invoice price = $1,000,000 \times (1 - d \times n/360)$ where d = Futures discount (100 − Discount Index)/100 n = Number of days from delivery to maturity
Minimum Price Change:	.01 in index value; called one *basis point* or one *tick*. Note that this basis point is a discount basis point, not a rate basis point. For $n = 90$, each basis point change in index

value results in a \$25 change in invoice price. This is the amount of variation margin resulting from a one basis point change in futures price.

Daily Price Limit:	Eliminated as of December 19, 1985.
Delivery Months:	March, June, September, December. Six successive contracts are generally traded at any point in time. Of these, perhaps the first three are reasonably liquid.
Delivery Days:	The first delivery day is the day during the delivery month on which (1) a new 13-week bill first settles and (2) an old, original issue one-year bill has 13 weeks left to maturity. These two events coincide only once during a given delivery month. Delivery can be made on the three successive days starting on this day.
Adjustments for Delivery of Nonnominal Securities:	The invoice price calculation adjusts for n = 90, 91, or 92. Variation margin is paid assuming 90 days.
Trading Hours:	7:20 a.m. to 2:00 p.m. Central time.
Arbitrage Possibilities:	It is possible to do a cash and carry up to three delivery months out.
Break-Even Repo Rate:	The *BERR* for bills is an algebraic rearrangement of Equations 3-2 and 3-7:

T-bill futures $BERR =$ (3-15)

$$\frac{(d' \times n'/360) - (d \times n/360)}{1 - (d' \times n'/360)} \times \frac{360}{n' - n}$$

where

d = Futures discount (100 − Index)/100

n = Number of days from delivery to maturity

d' = Current discount on cash bill

n' = Number of days from next cash settlement date to maturity

Remember that the repo rate and break-even repo rate are on a 360-day year basis.

Cheapest Deliverable:
All deliverable bills are likely to be equally cheap to deliver.

Duration:
The duration of the futures contract is the duration of the bill most likely to be delivered (normally a 90- or 91-day bill):

$$91/365 = .25$$

Basis Point Value:
$$BPV = 24.66 \times (1 - .25 \times d)^{5.056} \qquad (3\text{-}16)$$

This is the change in futures invoice price for a one basis point change in the annually compounded rate. The semiannually compounded BPV is

$$BPV = 24.66 \times (1 - .25 \times d)^{3.028} \qquad (3\text{-}17)$$

Variation margin is always paid assuming n equals 90, and an n of 90 is assumed in equations 3-16 and 3-17. Note that a one basis point change in the rate is not to be confused with a one basis point change in the discount index, which always results in a $25 margin flow.

Comments:
Delivery typically occurs on the first possible date since carry costs generally are equal to or greater than discount accreted until later delivery. There is a substantial chance that arbitragers doing a reverse cash and carry in T-bills will fail on part of the transaction, since they will have to pay for delivery by 12:00 noon Central time, whereas their reverse repo may not by terminated until later in the day. Because of the way delivery dates are determined for T-bill futures, the delivered bill under one contract does not typically mature on the delivery date of the following quarter's contract.

Thus, stripping in the literal sense explored in Chapter 2 is not possible in T-bill futures. In practice, however, stripping can be used to create something very similar to synthetic long-term Treasury security.

Contract:	**Eurodollar Time Deposit**
Symbol:	ED
Exchange:	International Monetary Market (IMM), a division of the Chicago Mercantile Exchange.
Deliverable Security:	There is no delivery made on Eurodollar futures (Euros). A final trading day settlement price is determined by the Merc based on LIBOR rates as follows: From a list of 20 participating London banks, twelve are selected and asked their 90-day LIBOR at a random time within the last 90 minutes of trading. The two high and the two low quotes are discarded, the remaining eight are averaged, and the expiring futures price is set to 100 minus the average. A final margin flow occurs, and the contract expires.
Size of Delivery Unit:	The price is designed to reflect the value of a 90-day Eurodollar time deposit with a principal value of $1,000,000.
Pricing System:	Add-on index for futures. Refer to Equations 4-3 to 4-5.
Invoice Price Calculation:	Since there is no delivery, there is no invoice calculation.
Minimum Price Change:	.01 in index value; called one *basis point*, or *tick*. Each basis point change in index price results in $25 in margin flows.
Daily Price Limit:	Eliminated as of December 19, 1985.
Delivery Months:	March, June, September, and December.

Contracts up to three years form expiration can be traded at any given time.

Delivery Days: The last settlement date is the second London business day immediately preceding the third Wednesday of the contract month. Trading terminates at 3:30 p.m. London time.

Trading Hours: 7:20 a.m. to 2:00 p.m. Central time.

Arbitrage Possibilities: No delivery means no arbitrage opportunities. Quasi-arbitrage remains possible.

Duration: Because the deliverable security is hypothetical, duration always equals 90/365 or .2466.

Basis Point Value: $$BPV = 24.66/(1 + .25 \times r_a)^{3.06} \qquad (3\text{-}18)$$
annually compounded, or

$$BPV = 24.66/(1 + .125 \times r_a)^{1.03} \qquad (3\text{-}19)$$
semiannually compounded
where
$r_a = (100 - \text{futures price})/100.$

This BPV is the margin flow which results from a one basis point change in the annually or semiannually compounded, 365-day market rate. The 360-day, add-on rate changes a little less than one basis point for each basis point change in the annually compounded, 365-day rate.

Comments: Quasi-arbitrage activity causes this contract to trade very efficiently up to three or more quarters from expiration. Later contracts tend to trade a bit cheap relative to cash LIBOR rates. The advent of Eurodollar futures options has increased liquidity in the contract.

LIBOR is the rate at which institutions offer to invest in Eurodollar time deposits, and LIBID is the rate that institutions are willing to pay to attract time deposits. In examining quasi-arbitrage situations requiring long futures positions to hedge the yields on future Eurodollar investments, the LIBOR implied by the futures price should be reduced by an eighth of a percent to reflect a corresponding LIBID.

Contract:	**Five-Year Treasury Note Futures**
Symbol:	FY
Exchange:	FINEX Division of the New York Cotton Exchange
Deliverable Security:	Nominally, a Treasury note with original maturity between 4.5 and 5.5 years and between 4.25 and 5.5 years from delivery to maturity, with an annual coupon of 8%. With an adjustment to the invoice price, notes of appropriate maturity with any coupon can be delivered.
Size of Delivery Unit:	The face value of the delivered notes must equal $100,000. Notes delivered under any one contract must be of the same issue.
Pricing System:	Modified percent of par. A fifth digit is appended to the quoted price to denote tenths of a thirty-second of a percent of par; for example, 97-045 denotes 97 and 4.5 thirty-seconds. See Equations 4-1 and 4-2.
Invoice Price Calculation:	Invoice price = $100,000 × conversion factor × % of par futures price/100 + accrued coupon income.
Minimum Price Change:	1/64th of 1% of par. A 1/64th percent change in the futures price results in a $100,000 × .00015625 = $15.625 change in invoice price of the nominally deliverable note. Variation margin always is $15.625 per 64th change in the futures price.
Daily Price Limits:	None.
Delivery Months:	March, June, September, and December.

Delivery Days:	Delivery can be made on any business day of the delivery month up to the last business day of the month. Trading continues up 1:00 p.m. Eastern time on the eighth last business day of the delivery month. Notice of intent to deliver may be given as early as the second-last business day before the start of the delivery month and as late as the third last business day. Notice of intent to deliver may be given until 6:00 p.m. Eastern time and will result in an invoice price based on the closing futures price. Giving notice of intent to deliver initiates a three-day delivery procedure. The following day a long position holder is assigned for delivery and short invoices long. On day three, note ownership is transferred to the long position holder in book-entry form and funds are sent to the short via Fed Funds wire.
Trading Hours:	8:30 a.m. to 3:00 p.m. Eastern time.
Adjustments for Nonnominal Deliveries:	Conversion factors are calculated to adjust for delivery of notes with coupons other than 8%.

The following formula which generates the officially used conversion factors:

Let

$$f = \frac{C}{8} - \left(\frac{C}{8} - 1\right) \times \frac{1}{1.04^{\mathrm{Int}(2 \times M)}} \qquad (3\text{-}20a)$$

where

C = Annual coupon rate in percent

M = Years from the 15th of the delivery month to maturity, rounded down to the nearest whole month

$\mathrm{Int}(X) = X$ rounded down to the nearest whole number.

If the quantity $2 \times M$ is an integer (whole

number), then f equals the conversion factor. Otherwise, the conversion factor is

$$CF = \frac{f + C/200}{1.04^{.5}} - \frac{C}{400} \qquad (3\text{-}20b)$$

The latter formula makes a rough adjustment for interest accrual between coupon payments.

Break-Even Repo Rate:

$$BERR = \frac{P_F \times CF + AI' - (P_C + AI)}{P_C + AI} \times \frac{360}{n}$$

$$(3\text{-}21)$$

where

P_F = Futures price (percent of par)

P_C = Cash price (percent of par)

CF = Conversion factor

AI = Accrued coupon income as of cash note purchase date

AI' = Accrued coupon income as of futures delivery

AI' = Accrued coupon income as of futures delivery date

n = Number of days from purchase to delivery of cash note

The *BERR* formula is not accurate for a cash and carry in which a coupon is paid during the holding period. In that case, some assumption must be made about the interest rate at which the coupon payment can be reinvested until delivery.

Effects of Conversion Factors on Arbitrage and Hedging:

Conversion factors complicate arbitrage relationships, since the invoice price for delivery of a particular note varies by

$$CF \times \Delta FP \times \$31.25$$

whereas margin variation, which always assumes the nominally deliverable note, only equals

$$\Delta FP \times \$31.25$$

Where

CF = The conversion factor of the cash note

ΔFP = The change in the note futures price, in ticks.

$31.25 = The value of a one tick change in futures price.

To lock in an effective invoice price in a cash and carry, arbitragers must sell CF futures contracts for each $100,000 face value note they intend to deliver. Just prior to delivery, they must offset $CF - 1$ futures per cash note and then deliver the cash notes into the remaining futures contracts. Similarly, in hedging or trading applications, the futures positions involved should be multiplied by the conversion factor of the cheapest deliverable note in calculating the hedge ratio (ratio of futures to cash notes in a hedged position).

Basis Point Value and Duration:	As described for coupon securities in Chapter 1; with modifications as follows: • set the price to futures price $\times$ conversion factor • set the settlement date to the futures delivery date.

Contract:	**Ten-Year Treasury Note Futures**
Symbol:	TY
Exchange:	Chicago Board of Trade
Deliverable Security:	Nominally, a Treasury note with between 6.5 and 10 years to maturity, with an annual coupon of 8%. With an adjustment to the invoice price, notes of appropriate maturity with any coupon can be delivered.

Pricing System: Percent of par. See Equations 4-1 and 4-2.

Invoice Price Calculation: Invoice price = $100,000 × conversion factor × % of par futures price/100 plus accrued coupon income.

Minimum Price Change: 1/32nd of 1% of par, also called one tick. One tick equals a $100,000 × .0003125 = $31.25 change in invoice price of the nominally deliverable note. Variation margin always is $31.25 per tick change in the futures price.

Daily Price Limits: Normally, 3% of par. If contracts for three or more delivery months move to the normal pricing limits, the limits are expanded to 150 percent of normal for the following three days. The Board of Trade has applied to the CFTC to expand normal daily limits to 4% of par.

Delivery Months: March, June, September, and December. Contracts can be traded up to eight delivery months out, although typically only the first three contracts are liquid.

Delivery Days: Delivery can be made on any business day of the delivery month. Trading continues up to 12:00 Noon Central time on the eighth last business day of the delivery month. Notice of intent to deliver may be given as early as two business days before the start of the delivery month and as late as the third last business day of the month (inclusive). Notice of intent to deliver must be given by 8:00 p.m. Central time and will result in a futures invoice price based on the closing futures price. Giving notice initiates a three day delivery process. On day two, the oldest outstanding long position is identified and invoices are sent to the long position holder by the short deliverer. On day three, the delivered notes are transferred to the long via book entry and funds are sent to the short via Fed Funds wire.

er. On day three, the delivered notes are transferred to the long via book entry and funds are sent to the short via Fed Funds wire.

Trading Hours: 8:00 a.m. to 2:00 p.m.

Adjustments for Nonnominal Deliveries: Conversion factors are calculated to adjust for delivery of notes with coupons other than 8%.

A formula which generates the officially used conversion factors is as follows:

Let

$$f = \frac{C}{8} - \left(\frac{C}{8} - 1\right) \times \frac{1}{1.04^{\text{Int}(2 \times M)}} \qquad (3\text{-}20a)$$

where

C = Annual coupon rate in %

M = Years from the first delivery day to maturity, rounded down to the nearest whole quarter

Int(X) = X rounded down to the nearest whole number.

If the quantity $2 \times M$ is an integer (whole number), then f equals the conversion factor. Otherwise, the conversion factor is

$$CF = \frac{f + C/200}{1.04^{.5}} - \frac{C}{400} \qquad (3\text{-}20b)$$

The latter formula makes a rough adjustment for interest accrual between coupon payments.

Break-Even Repo Rate: $$BERR = \frac{P_F \times CF + AI' - (P_C + AI)}{P_C + AI} \times \frac{360}{n}$$
$$(3\text{-}21)$$

where

P_F = Futures price (percent of par)

P_C = Cash price (percent of par)

CF = Conversion factor

AI' = Accrued coupon income as of futures delivery date

n = Number of days from purchase to delivery of cash note

The *BERR* formula is not accurate for a cash-and-carry in which a coupon is paid during the holding period. In that case, some assumption must be made about the interest rate at which the coupon payment can be reinvested until delivery.

Effects of Conversion Factors on Arbitrage and Hedging: Conversion factors complicate arbitrage relationships, since the invoice price for delivery of a particular note varies by

$$CF \times \Delta FP \times \$31.25$$

whereas margin variation, which always assumes the nominally deliverable note, only equals

$$\Delta FP \times \$31.25$$

where

CF = The conversion factor of the cash note

ΔFP = The change in the note futures price, in ticks.

$\$31.25$ = The value of a one tick change in futures price.

To lock in an effective invoice price in a cash and carry, arbitragers must sell CF futures contracts for each $100,000 face value note they intend to deliver. Just prior to delivery, they must offset $CF - 1$ futures per cash note, and then deliver the cash notes into the remaining futures contracts. Similarly, in hedging or trading applications, the futures positions involved should be multiplied by the conversion factor of the cheapest deliverable note in calculating the hedge ratio (ratio of futures to cash notes in a hedged position).

Basis Point Value and Duration:
As described for coupon securities in Chapter 1, with modifications as follows:
- set the price to futures price × conversion factor
- set the settlement date to the futures delivery date.

Potential changes in the cheapest-to-deliver note, specials in the repo market, and other factors may cause T-note futures to trade more cheaply than the expected note price as of delivery. For this reason, you may wish to plug a reasonable repo rate into the *BERR* formula and back out a fair futures price. Use this fair futures price in calculating BPV and duration.

Contract: **Treasury Bond**

Symbol: US

Exchange: Chicago Board of Trade

Deliverable Security: Nominally, a Treasury bond not callable earlier than 15 years from delivery of the futures contract, and carrying a coupon of 8%. With an adjustment to invoice price, any bond with a maturity greater than 15 years from delivery to the earlier of call or maturity may be delivered.

Size of Delivery Unit: The face value of the delivered bonds must equal $100,000. Bonds delivered under any one contract must be of the same issue.

All Other Features: Same as for Treasury Note futures.

Comments: An arbitrage analogous to the cash and carry is possible by buying a nearby futures contract and selling a later contract. Thus a liquid market in spreads exists for delivery months as far out as three years.

Some of the bonds which are deliverable into the bond futures contract are callable five years before their final maturity. If a callable bond is cheapest to deliver, *BPV* should be calculated assuming that the bond will be called if it is selling significantly above par. If it is selling at par, a date between the call and maturity dates can be used.

Contract:	**Long-Term Municipal Bond Index Futures**
Symbol:	MB
Exchange:	Chicago Board of Trade
Deliverable Security:	The Municipal Bond Index futures are for cash settlement only; no delivery is possible.

On the eighth last business day of the delivery month, the contract is marked to the value of the Bond Buyer Municipal Bond Index. The index is a multiple of a simple average of factored prices of the 40 most actively traded municipal bonds meeting index criteria.

Bonds eligible for inclusion in the index are issues of $50 million or more ($75 million or more for housing bonds), rated A or better by Moody's or a- or better by Standard and Poor's, with 19 or more years to maturity and callable at par between seven and 16 years. Additional criteria stipulate that the reoffer or reissuance price must fall between 95 and 105% of par and that the Bond Buyer may elect to include no more than two bonds from a single issuer in the index.

Conversion factors for bonds included in the index are calculated in the same way as factors for Treasury notes and bonds, to standardize the bonds to an 8% yield from the expiration date of the futures contract to the bond's first call. In calculating the index, the market prices of the bonds are divided by their conversion factors, the resulting 40 factored prices are summed and divided by 40, and the result is multiplied by a coefficient.

Every two weeks, bonds which are more actively traded than those included in the index are added to the index, and a corresponding number of the least active issues in the index are dropped. To prevent discontinuities in the index on changeover dates, the index is multiplied by a coefficient equal to the old index value divided by the new index value.

The index value is calculated daily 15 minutes before the close of trading. Five municipal bond firms estimate the current market price of each index bond; the high and low estimates are dropped and the remaining three are averaged to determine the bond price to be used in calculation of the index. The index calculation is released at approximately 2:30 p.m. Central time each day. During the delivery month, the index is calculated twice each day, at 10:45 a.m. as well as at 1:45 p.m. Central time and is released around 11:30 a.m. and 2:30 p.m.

Size of Delivery Unit:	$100,000 face value.
Pricing System:	Percent of par, fractions in 32nds.
Minimum Price Change:	One 32nd of 1% of par or one tick. One tick change in the futures price results in $31.25 in variation margin.
Daily Price Limits:	3% of par. If contracts for three or more delivery months trade at the limit, limits for the next trading day are expanded to 150% of normal for the next three days.
Delivery Months:	March, June, September, and December.
Expiration Day:	The eighth last business day of the delivery month.

Daily Price Limits:	3% of par. If contracts for three or more delivery months trade at the limit, limits for the next trading day are expanded to 150% of normal for the next three days.
Delivery Months:	March, June, September, and December.
Expiration Day:	The eighth last business day of the delivery month.
Trading Hours:	8:00 a.m. to 2:00 p.m. Central time.
BPV:	The BPV of the Muni bond contract is difficult to determine with precision because of the complexity of the Bond Buyer Index (BBI), and because the futures price often takes wide excursions from fair value as measured by most methods. A simplified procedure which will yield reasonable result follows:

1. Determine the price and coefficient of the Bond Buyer Index and the average coupon, average price, and average call date for the cash bonds included in the BBI.

2. Calculate an average conversion factor for the Index:

$$\text{Avg. } CF = \text{Avg. price/BBI} \times \text{coefficient}$$
(3-22a)

3. Calculate a fair average forward price for the bonds in the BBI:

$$\text{Fwd. Avg. Price} = \text{Avg. Price} \times$$
$$(1 + (r - y) \times 360/n)$$
(3-22b)

where

r = carry rate
y = average coupon of cash bonds in BBI, divided by Avg. price.

4. Calculate a raw basis point value for a

hypothetical coupon security with a price equal to the fair forward price calculated in Step 3, a coupon equal to the average coupon of the bonds in the BBI, and a maturity date equal to the average call date of the bonds in the BBI.

5. Calculate the factored BPV of the futures:

Futures BPV =

$$\text{Raw BPV} \times \frac{\text{coefficient}}{\text{avg. conv. factor}}$$

Comments: The Muni bond contract appears to be successful as a means to buy and sell the market in tax-exempt securities and through spread trades to exploit anticipated changes in tax laws. The contract has great potential as a hedge tool, although currently the futures prices take long excursions from theoretically fair levels. As the contract matures and becomes more deeply liquid, actual and theoretical prices should more closely match. Until then, their mispricing represents both opportunity and peril to the prospective tax exempt hedger.

Conclusion

The futures contracts you are likely to use in managing your particular rate risk exposures generally obey the principles discussed in Chapter 2. Their behavior is also influenced by quirks in their design and in the design of the markets for deliverable cash securities. While many of these esoteric wrinkles in contract specification are only important to arbitragers, some have a significant enough influence on futures price behavior to warrant study by arbitragers and hedgers alike. In contemplating the use of a particular futures contract, take some time to learn the specifications of the contract to see which design features might have an impact on you.

In Chapter 4, we shall see examples of typical uses of futures to eliminate or modify rates risk in a variety of real-world contexts. You will notice in all the examples the importance of familiarity with pricing systems, adjustments for substitutions, and the implications of the pricing principle in creating successful hedges or trades.

CHAPTER 4

Futures Applications

This chapter provides some examples of the principal uses of futures applied to real-world rate risk management problems:

- Protecting asset value.
- Capturing a rate of return.
- Stabilizing a cost of funds.

The method used in the first few examples is basis point value matching with judgmental attention paid to the risk of nonparallel yield curve shifts. This method will suffice for many, and perhaps most, rate risk management problems. Two complications which necessitate the use of other techniques are large, unavoidable yield curve risk and substantial default risk. Through examples and discussion, the latter part of this chapter illustrates and explains strategies to deal with these complications.

Basis point value matching, whether for stabilizing value, return, or funding cost, involves one basic procedure:

1. Measure the interest sensitivity (*BPV*) of the existing asset or liability
2. Determine the *BPV* of the desired asset or liability
3. Select a futures contract to use and measure its *BPV*.
4. Establish a futures position such that

BPV of hedged asset or liability
+ *BPV* of futures position
_____
BPV of desired position.

In choosing a futures contract to use, a hedger should bear in mind that it is best to buy what is cheap and sell what is dear, all else being equal. If his sole objective is to minimize risk, he should choose a futures contract with risk and cash flow timing similar to those of the asset or liability to be hedged. Finally, the pricing principle will generally prevail: Similar securities earn similar rates of return. When a hedger adds *BPV* to his position, it behaves more like a long-term asset or liability; the rate associated with the position will resemble a longer-term rate. When a hedger reduces his position's *BPV,* the associated rate will look more like a short-term interest rate.

Protecting Asset Value

Consider this situation: On February 14, 1986 a fund manager has $10 million of Treasury bills maturing on September 4, 1986. She intend to sell the bills sometime during the coming week. Interest rates have been volatile, and the fund manager is concerned that the bills will decline in value before their sale. How can she protect their value?

The solution is to *short hedge*—to establish a futures position with a *BPV* negative to that of the cash bill position. The change in asset value will then be offset exactly by variation margin from the futures for any parallel rate shift; the value of the bills is protected until the fund manager sells them. The actual calculations used to design this short hedge are as follows:

Asset

Type: T-bills   Discount: .0707

Maturity: 9/04/86

The first step is to calculate the basis point value of the cash bills to be hedged. From Equation 3-10, we show that the bill's annually compounded rate of return is

$$\left[\frac{1}{1 - .0707 \times 201/360}\right]^{(365/201)} - 1 = .0759.$$

Their dollar price per million (from Equation 3-7) is

$$1,000,000 \times [1 - (.0707 \times 201)/360] = 960,526.$$

Using Equation 1-5, the basis point value per million is

$$960,526 \times \frac{.0001}{1.0759} \times \frac{201}{365} = 49.16.$$

The $10MM in bills would decline in value a total of $491.60 were rates to rise .01%.

The next step in hedging the bills is to choose an appropriate futures contract to sell short. A logical choice is the June 1986 Treasury bill futures contract. The cash bills are deliverable into this futures contract, and, therefore, carry costs are the sole force affecting the relationship between them. The futures discount index is at 93.23, corresponding to a forward discount of .0677. Having chosen a futures contract, basis point value is calculated using Equation 3-16:

$$24.66 \times (1 - .0677 \times 90/360)^{(1+365/90)} = 22.61.$$

For a .01% rise in rates, a short futures contract produces a margin inflow of $22.61. The final step in designing the hedge is to determine what number of futures contracts will have a *BPV* that exactly offsets the *BPV* of the cash bills. Per million dollars face value of the cash bills, this will require

$$\frac{\text{Cash } BPV}{\text{Futures } BPV} = \frac{\$49.16}{\$22.61} = 2.17 \text{ contracts}$$

A short position of 22 June 1986 bill futures would be established to hedge the $10 million cash bill inventory.

Results

The hedge the fund manager established on February 14 was offset on February 19, when the cash bills were sold. At that point, the discount on the cash bills stood at .0712 and the futures index was 93.17.

If the discount had not changed, the cash bills would have been worth

$$\$1,000,000 \times (1 - .0707 \times 196/360) = \$961,508,$$

whereas with a discount of .0712, they were worth

$1,000,000 × (1 − .0712 × 196/360) = $961,236,

for a loss of $272 per million face value.

The futures contracts gained (93.23 − 93.17) × 2500 × 2.2 = $330.00 per million. $4.50 of this gain was due to using 2.2 rather than 2.17 contracts per million; an exact hedge would have yielded a $325.50 per million gain on the futures position.

Assuming a precise hedge ratio, the return earned on the bills over a five day period was:

$$\left[\frac{\$961,236 + 325.50}{\$960,526}\right]^{(365/5)} - 1 = .0818.$$

Notice that the forward rate reflected in the bill futures price was below the return to maturity of the hedged cash bills. This implies that the yield curve was inverted over the relevant range at the start of the hedge. By hedging the bills to a net *BPV* of zero, the fund manager effectively made them into an overnight asset. Consistent with the pricing principle, the hedged position earned an overnight rate of return which was higher than the return to maturity of the hedged cash bills. Compare this return to the return on the unhedged cash position:

$$\left[\frac{\$961,236}{\$960,526}\right]^{(365/5)} - 1 = .0554.$$

The question naturally arises: Would this result have obtained under any possible rate scenario? A steepening or flattening of the yield curve would have resulted in a gain or loss on the hedge, and thus an experienced rate of return different from the overnight rate which prevailed during the hedge period. The hedged cash bills lie on the first seven months of the yield curve, while the bill futures lie on months four to seven. A change in rates which affects the first three months on the yield curve differently than months four to seven would thus affect the hedge's performance.

Stabilizing a Rate of Return

Let's consider another scenario. Suppose an insurance company has made a ten-year loan at a fixed rate of 9.5 percent. The loan calls for a bullet payment of $70 million interest plus principal at maturity. The loan is match funded with a ten-year liability on the insurer's books.

On January 3, 1986, the borrower asks to prepay the loan without penalty in mid-March. Past experience suggests the insurer can lend with acceptable credit risk at 110% of government rates; in this environment, 8.18% for a 10-week loan and 10.16% for a ten-year loan, on a semiannual basis.

In the current rate environment, the insurer could increase return by permitting prepayment and relending at higher prevailing rates. Having committed to allowing the prepayment, the insurer cannot count on present rates persisting until the prepayment occurs in 10 weeks. Using a *long hedge* in the futures market, however, the insurer could in a sense lock in the current rate environment until the prepayment is due.

Conceptually, by permitting prepayment the insurer has converted the loan from a ten-year asset to a 10-week asset, but still wishes to have a ten-year asset earning current market rates. By purchasing a futures contract on a 9.81-year security to be delivered in ten weeks, the insurer could use the prepayment proceeds to buy the delivered security at a known price. The prepayment and the futures together constitute a synthetic asset, or *strip,* of cash and futures with a maturity of ten years. Generally, using futures to add *BPV* to an existing cash position creates a synthetic asset with longer-term asset characteristics.

Designing a long hedge for the insurance company loan, requires the following calculations:

First, the loan prepayment must be quantified. The present value of $70 million in 9.81 years (using the contractually stipulated rate of 9.5%) is

$$\frac{\$70,000,000}{(1 + .095/2)^{(2\times9.81)}} = \$28,162,807.$$

This is the amount that will be prepaid. The market rate available on this 12-week asset is 8.18%; the *BPV* of the loan if prepayment is allowed is thus

$$\frac{\$28,162,807}{(1 + .08175/2)^{(2\times70/365)}} - \frac{28,162,807}{(1 + .08185/2)^{(2\times70/365)}} = \$511.$$

The asset the insurer wishes to own pays $70 million in ten years and earns the currently available ten-year rate of 10.16%. The *BPV* of the desired asset is

$$\frac{\$70,000,000}{(1 + .10155/2)^{(2 \times 10)}} - \frac{\$70,000,000}{(1 + .10165/2)^{(2 \times 10)}} = \$24,727.$$

Notice that in all cases, actual cash flows, market rates, and market-determined present values are used in basis point value calculations.

To create a long hedge, the insurer wishes to construct a futures position with a total *BPV* of

$$\$24,727 - \$511 = \$24,216.$$

Logically, the best futures contract to use will come as close as possible to delivering a 9.81-year asset ten weeks hence. The futures which comes closest to this is the ten-year note contract for delivery in March 1986.

The cheapest deliverable note is the 10.5% note maturing on August 15, 1995. The conversion factor for this note is 1.1610. The note futures price on January 2 is 92-22.

The invoice price of the 10.5% note, therefore, would be

$$\$92,688 \times 1.1610 = \$107,610 \text{ (excluding coupon accrual)}$$

per $100,000 face value. The yield to maturity from 3/21/86 to 8/15/95 of a 10.5% note costing $107,610 is 9.27%. A basis point value using this starting rate equals $65.03.

To capture a synthetic ten-year rate of return, the insurer must sell enough futures to add $24,216 in *BPV* to the existing cash position. If the *BPV* of the futures equals the *BPV* of the cheapest deliverable note, $65.03, it is intuitively appealing to say that the hedge would consist of

$$\frac{\$24,216}{\$65.03} = 371.38 \text{ contracts.}$$

However, this hedge position does not adjust for two important factors. First, remember that the invoice price of the cheapest deliverable note changes by the conversion factor times the change in the futures price.

In contrast, variation margin is paid assuming that the nominally deliverable note will be delivered. To compensate for this quirk, the hedge position must be multiplied by the conversion factor, 1.1610. The hedge ratio becomes

$$\frac{\$24,216}{\$65.03} \times 1.1610 = 432.34 \text{ contracts.}$$

A final adjustment to the hedge is intended to compensate for the fact that the market rate available to the insurance company consistently equals 110% of government rates. The above hedge thus should be grossed up by a factor of 1.1, to

$$432.34 \times 1.1 = 475.57 \text{ or } 476 \text{ contracts.}$$

This factor of 1.1 is sometimes referred to as a *risk beta*, because it is designed to adjust hedges of (default) risky cash securities with futures on riskless government issues, and because *beta* is a term borrowed from the regression techniques used to estimate risk betas. Risk betas are not a flawless tool, as will be discussed later in this chapter.

Results

When the hedge was established, the forward rate between ten weeks and ten years equaled 10.20%. The objective of the hedge was to ensure that in mid-March the insurance company could lend $26,378,661 at 10.20% for 9.81 years, receiving $70 million of interest and principal at maturity. On March 14, the rate at which the new loan was booked was 8.76, or 110% of the prevailing ten-year note of 7.96%. At this rate, principal of $30,187,473 had to be loaned to result in the same $70 million cash flow at maturity, reflecting an opportunity cost to the insurance company of $3,808,812.

The price of the March 1986 note futures rose from 92-22 to 101-05 over the same period, resulting in variation margin of $4,031,125, and covering 106% of the opportunity cost experienced on the loan due to declining rates.

These results could have been affected favorably or adversely by a variety of factors, including a change in the cheapest deliverable note, changes in term repo rates, or, most importantly, changes in the relationship between Treasury rates and the rates at which the insurance company could lend. Had the change in the insurance company's lending rate been 112% of the change in ten-year Treasury yields, the hedge results would not have been as favorable. This situation could have occurred due to a twist in the yield curve, since the loan has a duration of 9.81 years, while the note futures' duration is just over six years. A change in the market's perception of the risk of this kind of lending would have affected the attainable lending rate as well.

Creating a Synthetic Asset

In the previous example, the objective essentially was to hedge the price of an asset to be purchased on a future date. A related strategy is to create a synthetic asset composed of cash securities and futures, which mimics the risk characteristics of a natural cash security, but which, by exploiting inefficient market pricing, yields a superior return.

An investor in Eurodollar time deposits should investigate the possibility of creating synthetic time deposits. Consider the investor who wishes to buy a ten-month Eurodollar time deposit. On November 9, 1987, 308-day time deposits offer a return of 7.625%. The investor focuses on this particular maturity because he knows that a synthetic 308-day time deposit can be constructed by purchasing a 37-day cash time deposit and the December 1987, March 1988 and June 1988 Eurodollar futures contracts. After 37 days, the investor reinvests in a three-month time deposit, the return on which is hedged by the December Eurodollar contract. When the three-month time deposit matures, the investor rolls the proceeds into a new three-month deposit, which is hedged by the June futures, and so on.

The final value of a dollar invested in the 308-day cash time deposit is

$$\$1 \times (1 + .07625 \times 308/360) = \$1.065236.$$

The synthetic alternative can be evaluated as follows. A 37-day Eurodollar time deposit yields 6.82% The futures contracts are trading at the prices tabled below:

Contract	Price	LIBOR	Implied LIBID*
EDZ87	92.57	7.43	7.305
EDH88	92.40	7.60	7.475
EDM88	92.04	7.96	7.835

*Assumes LIBID 1/8% below LIBOR, a typical spread.

The final value of $1 invested in the synthetic alternative is

$$\$1 \times (1 + .0682 \times 37/360) \times (1 + .07305 \times 91/360)$$
$$\times (1 + .07475 \times 91/360) \times (1 + .07835 \times 91/360) = 1.06568.$$

Converting to an annualized add-on rate:

Cash time deposit: .065236 × 360/308 = .07625
Synthetic: .065680 × 360/308 = .07677

Synthetic advantage: .07677 − .07625   = .0052 or 5.2 basis points.

In the prevailing market environment, the advantage to the synthetic investment alternative is modest. The methods used work equally well in revealing less modest opportunities when they arise.

Stabilizing a Cost of Funds

A bank lending officer's prospective customer is seeking funds to finance a project. The customer will require a $1 million initial drawdown and additional takedowns of $1 million per quarter at the beginnings of the next seven quarters. The total borrowings of $8 million plus interest will be paid at the end of the last quarter, when the project will be sold to a third party. The prospective customer wants to find fixed-rate financing for the project, since financing costs could make the difference between profit or loss. None of the customer's other banks are willing to lend at fixed rates and have instead offered to lend at Prime (floating). The lender officer is in the same position, but is determined to gain the prospective customer's business.

The solution is to offer a loan at a spread over LIBOR re-priced quarterly, and some advice. The lender advises the customer to stabilize the projects' funding costs with a hedge in the

Eurodollar futures market. The customer's rate risk is minimized; as long as the lending officer's bank can fund loans at a rate stably related to LIBOR, its profit spread is assured.

In describing an appropriate hedge strategy to the customer, the lender may wish to avoid discussing duration, BPV-matching or other such esoterica. Instead, the lender might wish to explain the hedge diagrammatically, as shown in Figures 4-1 through 4-3.

In fact, the number of futures contracts taken from the diagram will match very closely the number of contracts the lender would have estimated using BPV-matching. At the beginning of each quarter, the customer will borrow from the bank at a spread over the prevailing LIBOR, and so in effect will issue Eurodollar liabilities through the bank. The customer thus can short-sell Eurodollar time deposits forward in the futures market and know now what the total cost of funding the project will be.

It may not be possible to buy eight-quarter strips to fix the cost of borrowing, since the Eurodollar contract may not always be liquid eight quarters out. However, a short position of 35 contracts could be placed in any contract month and have the same effect with respect to parallel rate shifts. The principle "buy cheap, sell dear" applies here. If one contract month were very expensive (relative to the others or versus arbitrage relationships), it might be desirable to stack the short position in that contract month, even though such a strategy would expose the customer to twists in the yield curve. If no obviously overpriced contract exists, a partial strip in the five nearby contracts would approach the full strip depicted in Figure 4-4.

Over time, the hedge position will have to be reduced as the time left to maturity of the loan declines. Simply offsetting contracts just before expiration will approximate the required hedge adjustment. As contracts for delivery in quarters seven and eight become liquid, the stack in quarter six should be rolled into the later expiration month.

Maturity Cross-Hedging

Basis point value matching allows us to hedge any asset or liability using any futures contract, e.g. to hedge bonds in bills

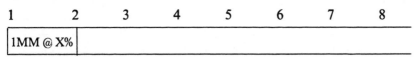

Figure 4-1 Commitment Customer Has as of First Takedown

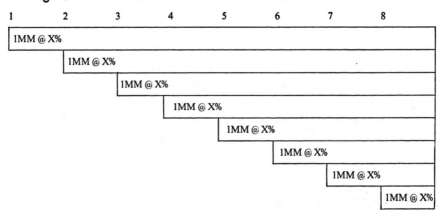

Figure 4-2 Commitment Customer Wants as of First Takedown

Figure 4-3 Solution: Customer Sells Eurodollar Futures as if Customer Could Issue and Deliver

1	2	3	4	5	6	7	8
	1 ctrct	1 ctrct	1 ctrct	1 ctrct	1 ctrct	1 ctrct	1 ctrct
	1 ctrct	1 ctrct	1 ctrct	1 ctrct	1 ctrct	1 ctrct	1 ctrct
		1 ctrct	1 ctrct	1 ctrct	1 ctrct	1 ctrct	1 ctrct
			1 ctrct	1 ctrct	1 ctrct	1 ctrct	1 ctrct
				1 ctrct	1 ctrct	1 ctrct	1 ctrct
					1 ctrct	1 ctrct	1 ctrct
						1 ctrct	1 ctrct
							1 ctrct

Total of 35 contracts

Figure 4-4 Partial Strip Hedge.

Delivery at beginning of quarter

1	2	3	4	5	6	7	8
	2 ctrcts	3 ctrcts	4 ctrcts	5 ctrcts	21 ctrcts	0 ctrcts	0 ctrcts

Total of 35 contracts

futures as well as bond futures. As long as the *BPV* of the futures position is the negative of the *BPV* of the hedged item, the combined position will be insulated against parallel shifts in the yield curve. Twists in the yield curve, on the other hand, may expose the futures to a different change in rates than the hedged item, causing the hedge to show a net profit or loss. In principle, unless the cash flows associated with the futures position exactly match the cash flows of the hedged item in size and timing, some change in the yield curve is possible which would cause the hedge to result in a net profit or loss.

A hedge in which the cash flows associated with the futures are different in size and timing from the cash flows associated with the hedged item is called a *maturity cross-hedge*. The vast majority of hedges created in practice involve some degree of maturity cross-hedging. Maturity cross-hedge performance is inherently vulnerable to nonparallel shifts in the yield curve. Conservative hedgers will wish to minimize the sensitivity of a maturity cross-hedge to twists in the yield curve, while more aggressive hedgers will still wish to control the degree of twist sensitivity to which they are exposed in a maturity cross-hedge.

Three additional examples illustrate the three strategies for controlling risk of nonparallel shifts in the yield curve when maturity cross-hedging is unavoidable: (1) hedging in a single futures contract; (2) subjective allocation of a hedge between more than one futures contract; and (3) the use of slope point value in a multiple contract hedge to insulate optimally against changes in the level and slope of the yield curve.

Single Contract Maturity Cross-Hedges

A prospective hedger owns ten-year notes. He has considered selling them to buy short-term securities, but believes that ten-year yields are anomalously high relative to thirty-year yields. He is dissatisfied with the price he could get by selling the notes, and feels that by hedging in note futures he would merely lock in the low price reflected in the cash yield curve. Instead, he elects to cross-hedge his cash notes using Treasury bond futures. In so doing, he eliminates the risk of parallel yield curve shifts, but deliberately remains sensitive to a change in the slope of the yield curve from the ten-to thirty-year region.

On June 26, he uses September bond futures to hedge $10 million of the 8 7/8 T-notes maturing on February 15, 1996. The cash notes are trading at 109-04% of par and the futures are at 98-11. The cheapest-to-deliver bond is the 14% of November 2011, callable in 2006. The hedge ratio is calculated the same as for a hedge in note futures.

Conversion factor of cheapest-to-deliver bond: 1.5938
BPV of bond futures: 150.75
BPV of 8 7/8 notes: 716.60
Number of contracts to hedge: 716.60/150.75 × 1.5938 = 7.58

To establish the hedge, 76 September 1986 bond futures are sold at 98.11.

On July 7, the hedger takes stock of his position. Marking to market, the 8 7/8 notes are trading at 109-28 and the September bond futures at 100-13. The futures loss is $156,750 and the gain in the cash notes value is $75,000. Because ten-year yields declined by less than thirty-year yields over the hedge period, the return to the position was negative. Had the hedger's expectations proven correct, and ten-year yields declined relative to thirty-year yields, the position would have shown a return above the overnight rate of return during the holding period (and in fact would have done so on several occasions after July 6).

Cross-Hedging with Two or More Contracts

A second hedger owns three-year notes she wishes to hedge. She has no opinion on the behavior of the yield curve and wishes to hedge as conservatively as possible. None of the contracts available to her would result in a completely satisfactory hedge; a hedge in bill futures would lose if the yield curve steepened, while a hedge in ten-year T-note futures would lose if the curve flattened.

A possible solution to this problem is to place a portion of the hedge in bill futures and a portion in note futures, bracketing the maturity of the cash notes being hedged. To do so, the hedger simply decides what fraction of the cash notes' *BPV* is to be hedged in bill futures and what fraction in note futures, the sum of the fractions being equal to one. The hedger calculates the quantity of contracts required to hedge the cash position entirely in bill futures and multiplies this quantity by the fraction of the hedge to be placed in the bill futures. The hedger then calculates the quantity of note futures required to hedge the cash position entirely in note futures and multiples this quantity by the fraction of the hedge to be placed in note futures.

Consider a hedge on April 21, 1986 of a portfolio of short-term notes. The hedger elects to hedge 70% in June 1986 bill futures and 30% in June 1986 note futures. The hedge is lifted on May 12. The hedge calculations are as follows:

Description	Face amount	4/21 price	BPV	5/21 price
9¾ of 1/87	$1,000,000	102-18	72.64	102-06
12⅜ of 1/88	$1,000,000	109-17	172.23	108-12
9⅝ of 11/90	$1,000,000	110-15	410.58	107-25
June T-bill futures		94.51	22.99	93.96
June ten year note futures		104-02	62.38*	99.25

*Factored cheapest: 11¼ of 5/95, C.F. = 1.2015.

TB position: .7 × 655.45/22.99 = 19.96 or 20 TBM
TY position: .3 × 655.45/62.38 = 3.15 or 3 TYM

Cash loss: $42,187   Futures gain: $40,344

Compare this to the futures gain for a cross-hedge in 29 June T-bill futures of $39,875, or in a cross-hedge solely in 11 June ten-year note futures of $47,094. Better coverage is provided by a combination hedge by a modest margin.

The hedger using this technique could have chosen any proportion of bills to notes or could have extended the technique to three, four, or more futures contracts. Her criteria for apportioning the hedge are subjective and rely on the intuition that any hedge in contracts which bracket the maturity of the hedged notes will outperform a single contract hedge in a nonparallel yield curve shift. The subjectivity of this approach begs a question. Is there a particular proportion of bill and note futures which will optimally insulate against parallel and nonparallel yield curve changes?

BPV and SPV Matched Hedging

Slope point value (SPV), introduced in Chapter 1, can be used to identify the optimal combination of bond and note futures to insulate the hedged asset from all changes in the level and slope of the yield curve. The resulting hedge would remain vulnerable to changes in the degree of curvature of the yield curve.

Slope point value is a more difficult procedure to use than basis point value, since securities must be broken down into component cash flows which are then analyzed one by one. The first step in using slope point is to observe the pure discount or *zero-coupon* (zero) yield curve. This curve might be taken from market-maker indications on TIGRs or CATs (nearly risk-free pure discount securities collateralized by Treasury security coupons), or might be estimated from actively traded Treasury security prices.

Having estimated the zero curve, the hedger can calculate the basis point value and slope point value of the cash notes using the actual zero curve rates, rather than YTM, as a proxy for the actual yield curve.

For each cash flow in the cash notes, the hedger observes the zero curve rate for the time until the cash flow is due, and measures the *BPV* of each cash flow using Equation 1-5a:

$$\text{Single cash flow } BPV = \frac{CF_t}{(1 + r_t)^T} \times \frac{.0001}{1 + r_t} \times T$$

where
CF_t = cash flow occurring in t years

r_t = zero curve rate for a pure discount security maturing t years

t = years to receipt of cash flow CF_t.

Summing the *BPV*s of the cash notes' cash flows, the hedger has calculated the *BPV* of the entire cash note position.

To gauge an approximate* slope point value, the hedger assumes that the zero curve has steepened by a linear function of t, say, .0001 × t. Calculate slope point value by substituting .0001 × t for .0001 in the above equation for each cash flow:

$$\text{Single cash flow } SPV = \frac{CF_t}{(1 + r_t)^t} \times \frac{.0001 \times t}{1 + r_t} \times t.$$

Summing the single cash flow *SPV*s, the hedger obtains the *SPV* of the cash notes.

The hedger must then calculate the BPV and SPV of the bill and note futures contracts. This process is complicated by the fact that the futures interest sensitivity is controlled by the level and change of forward rates, not of term rates. For each cash flow, then, the level of the forward rate from futures delivery to receipt of the cash flow must be calculated to get the cash flow's BPV. The change in term rates of .0001 × t must be calculated before SPV can be determined. The forward rate from time t_1 to time t_2 equals

$$_{t_1}r_{t_2} = \left[\frac{(1 + r_{t_2})^{t_2}}{(1 + r_{t_1})^{t_1}} \right]^{[1/(t_2 - t_1)]} - 1$$

and the change in this forward rate when the term yield curve changes by .0001 × t equals

$$\Delta_{t_1}r_{t_2} = \left[\frac{(1 + r_{t_2} + .0001 \times t_2)^{t_2}}{(1 + r_{t_1} + .0001 \times t_1)^{t_1}} \right]^{[1/(t_2 - t_1)]} - 1 - {}_{t_1}r_{t_2}$$

---

*Approximate because Equation 1-5a is perfectly accurate only for very small values of Δr.

where

r_{t_2} = the term rate for a cash flow due in t_2 years

r_{t_1} = the term rate for a cash flow due in t_1 years

$\Delta_{t_1} r_{t_2}$ = the change in the forward rate from t_1 to t_2 which results from a change in the term yield curve of $.0001 \times t$.

Assume that the bill futures are deliverable at time t_1 and that the deliverable bill matures 90 days later, at time t_2. Then the BPV of the futures equals

$$\text{BPV} = \frac{1,000,000}{(1 + {}_{t_1}r_{t_2})^{(90/365)}} \times \frac{.0001}{1 + {}_{t_1}r_{t_2}} \times .2466.$$

Alternatively, Equation 3-17 may be used. The two will differ to the extent that the pricing principle is not being perfectly enforced. The SPV of the bill futures equals

$$\text{SPV} = \frac{1,000,000}{(1 + {}_{t_1}r_{t_2})^{90/365}} \times \frac{\Delta_{t_1} r_{t_2}}{1 + {}_{t_1}r_{t_2}} \times .2466.$$

For the note futures, the BPV and SPV of each cash flow must be calculated:

$$\text{Single cash flow BPV} = \frac{CF_{t_2}}{(1 + {}_{t_1}r_{t_2})^{(t_2 - t_1)}} \times \frac{.0001}{1 + {}_{t_1}r_{t_2}} \times (t_2 - t_1)$$

$$\text{Single cash flow SPV} = \frac{CF_{t_2}}{(1 + {}_{t_1}r_{t_2})^{t_2 - t_1}} \times \frac{\Delta_{t_1} r_{t_2}}{1 + {}_{t_1}r_{t_2}} \times (t_2 - t_1)$$

where

CF_{t_2} = cash flow occurring at t_2

The single cash flow BPVs are summed to get the BPV of the note futures. The single cash flow SPVs are summed to get the SPV of the note futures.

The hedger is now ready to calculate the number of bill and note futures needed to hedge the cash notes against shifts and twists in the zero curve. Two constraints must be met:

$$Q_B \times BPV_B + Q_N \times BPV_N = -BPV_C$$
$$Q_B \times SPV_B + Q_N \times SPV_N = -SPV_C$$

Solving for Q_B:

$$Q_B = \frac{BPV_N \times SPV_C - BPV_C \times SPV_N}{BPV_B \times SPV_N - BPV_N \times SPV_B}.$$

where

Q_B = Number of bill futures contracts

Q_N = Number of note futures contracts

BPV_B = BPV of bill futures contracts

BPV_N = BPV of note futures contracts

BPV_C = BPV of cash note contracts

SPV_B = SPV of bill futures contracts

SPV_N = SPV of note futures contracts

SPV_C = SPV of cash notes contracts

The value of Q_B can then be plugged into one of the two constraint equations to solve for Q_N.

Cross-Hedging Default Risk

A second type of cross-hedging situation arises when a security subject to substantial default risk is being hedged using futures on default-riskless government securities. In this situation, a basis point value matching approach to hedging might in certain circumstances increase rather than mitigate risk.

One simple approach to default risk was illustrated in the second example of this chapter, concerning the insurance company loan. The loan was subject to default risk and so could be booked at a rate which exceeded Treasury yields. Long experience suggested that competitive loan rates equaled 110% of Treasury yields for comparable maturities. Because the 110% assumption held true, the use of a risk beta adjustment to the number of futures contracts used proved an effective solution to the problem of cross-hedging the loan in T-note futures.

Several factors can render the risk beta approach less effective:

- The risk characteristics of the hedged security may change. The security's issuer may enter riskier lines of business, or, may increase its leverage, or public perception of the risk in its existing lines of business may change. Thus a risk beta estimated using historical data may not accurately describe the future relationship between risky and risk-free rates.

- It is difficult to specify an accurate model of the relationship between risky and risk-free rates. The hedger who assumes that a simple, linear relationship exists between risky and risk-free rates when in fact the relationship is complex and nonlinear, may misestimate the immediate sensitivity of risky rates to changes in the risk-free rate, and may overlook the possibility that the relationship may change as rates do.

Under what circumstances might a hedge, even one incorporating a careful risk beta adjustment, result in a net increase in risk? Disturbingly, the circumstances may occur frequently—whenever default risk and rate risk are inversely correlated. Quite often the issuer of a risky security is able to service debt easily when the economy is booming, but experiences difficulties during recession. Interest rates tend to rise during a boom (as demand rises for funds to finance inventory and production capacity), but fall off during a recession as inventory is reduced and spending plans are scaled back.

Consider the effect on a hedger of a risky corporate note: As the economy peaks, the hedger sees rates edging up and decides to sell T-note futures to hedge the corporate note. The economy then slides into recession; rates fall, causing a loss on the futures, but increased risk of default depresses the price of the corporate notes. The hedger loses on both cash and futures, and the hedged position loses more value than the unhedged corporate bond.

Clearly, two risks must be hedged to avoid the above scenario, the risk of rising rates and the risk of economic decline. Treasury features hedge only rate risk. A second futures contract might be used to hedge economic risk, say S&P 500 futures, since stock prices tend to fall when economic activity declines. It is as difficult to create an intuitively compelling model which will quantify the number of S&P futures to use in a particular hedge as it is to specify an accurate risk beta model. Reasonable success has been achieved in some studies nonetheless by taking an explicitly empirical approach to estimating appropriate quantities of futures to use in a given hedge. Conclusions to be drawn from these studies include:

- High-quality (i.e., AAA) securities are not hedged much more effectively using equity and Treasury futures than by using Treasury futures alone.
- As credit quality deteriorates, hedge effectiveness is improved by the addition of more equity futures contracts to the hedge. However, beyond a point the addition of more equity futures is futile. Notes in imminent danger of default do not correlate well with either Treasury or equity futures.
- Diversified portfolios of risky debt are effectively hedged using index futures like the S&P 500; individual securities are not. Company-specific risks loom large in the pricing of the obligations of individual companies, but tend to cancel each other out in diversified portfolios. To hedge individual debt issues, it may prove more effective to use Treasury futures and a small short position in the issuer's stock to control company-specific default risk.

Conclusion

Chapter 4 has presented a number of numerical and conceptual examples of the use of futures to control rate risk in commonly occurring situations; for example, when securities are to be sold off before maturity, when assets need to be purchased, and when funding costs need to be assured. The examples not only illustrated the use of duration, BPV, and SPV to calculate hedge positions, but also the power of arbitrage analysis and the pricing principle to suggest strategies and inform our expectations about hedge performance. The complications introduced by the presence of yield curve and default risk also hint at limitations to the effective use of futures.

Chapter 5 discusses a different kind of rate risk management tool which as grown explosively in importance during the last several years because it solves some types of rate risk problems more reliably and cost effectively than futures. That tool is the *interest rate swap*. As we shall see, the analytical techniques needed to use this new tool effectively are duration, BPV, SPV, and the pricing principle—essentially the same ones we have used to understand and use futures.

CHAPTER 5

Interest Rate Swaps

Futures contracts become deliverable and expire. While futures contracts on more and more types of underlying securities have been introduced, there are still some types of rates (e.g., prime) which are not controlled using futures without substantial basis risk.

Swaps offer a way to control rate risk for very long time periods without having to roll expiring contracts, and swaps have been devised which can provide better control of certain basis risks than currently traded futures contracts can. Further, swaps sometimes can result in a lower cost of funds (or higher asset return) than cash market alternatives. For these reasons, the swap market has grown to enormous size and is characterized by rapid innovation and good liquidity.

This chapter explains the basic nature of interest rate swaps, and some of the conventions used in their design and implementation. Then it will describe techniques for evaluating swap cost effectiveness and the impact of swap use on the interest sensitivity of the user's balance sheet.

Counterparties' Complementary Risks

Swap agreements are entered into when the parties to the agreement—known as *counterparties*—face interest rate risks which are complementary. For example, consider Counterparty A who has the ability to issue long-term debt at attractive rates but who prefers to invest in short-term assets, and Counterparty

B, who can only borrow short term but who prefers to invest in long-term assets. Counterparty A might be a banker who issues notes and lends at LIBOR, and B might run a thrift who issues CDs in a local marketplace and originates fixed rate mortgages. The market's perceptions, established relationships, and specific expertise of both counterparties make it difficult for them to control risk by changing their asset/liability mix.

Counterparty A is hurt by a fall in rates, which will reduce his or her asset return but not the cost of funds. Counterparty B is hurt by rising rates, which will increase his or her funding costs but not the asset return. If each could trade liability cash flow patterns, they could offset each other's risks. A swap agreement permits them to do so.

The Swap Agreement

Counterparties A and B might enter into a swap agreement in which they essentially agree to pay the interest on each other's liabilities. A would become the *floating rate payor,* agreeing to pay interest on B's short-term liabilities which are rolled several times at varying rates over the life of the swap. B would become the *fixed rate payor,* agreeing to pay the interest on A's fixed rate debt over the life of the swap. Each counterparty retains responsibility for repayment of principal (and ultimate responsibility for interest) while involved in the swap. However, because A's fixed rate debt interest is covered by payments from B, while A pays interest on a series of B's short-term liabilities, the effect is that A now has the liability cash flow pattern of short-term liability. Because B's short-term liability costs is paid by A while B pays interest on A's fixed rate debt, B effectively has a liability cash flow pattern of a fixed rate, long-term liability. The effect of the swap is shown schematically in Figure 5-1.

Swap Design and Implementation

Swap agreements are most commonly made between a given counterparty and a swap dealer, rather than between both ultimate counterparties. The dealer acts as the immediate counterparty to, for example, a fixed-rate payor, taking on the risk of a floating-rate payor and hedging that risk temporarily via futures or other means. The dealer then seeks a party wishing to become

Figure 5-1 Simple Interest Rate Swap

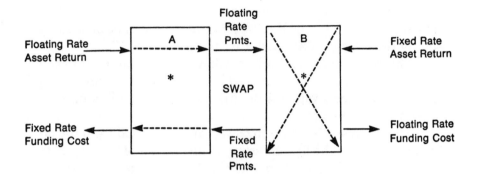

*Profit spread without rate risk. Each counterparty retains principal risk.

a floating-rate payor and enters into a second swap agreement, resulting in a matched book of fixed and floating inflows and outflows. The dealer provides liquidity and assures counterparty default risk with respect to both the ultimate fixed-rate and floating-rate payors. In return, the dealer exacts a small profit spread of several basis points by, for example, offering the floating-rate payor a slightly smaller fixed payment stream than the dealer takes in from the fixed-rate payor.

The size of the interest payments to be swapped are based on the size or notional amount of the liabilities generating the interest floats. Note that swap counterparties do not trade liabilities, but only the interest payment on their liabilities.

The counterparties to a swap typically are reluctant to swap interest expense regardless of the size of that expense. A floating-rate payor would be dismayed to assume a fixed-rate payor's short-term liability expenses, and then find that those expenses doubled because of a deterioration in the fixed-rate payor's credit worthiness. Therefore, the rate paid by the counterparties is tied to objective and easily-observed market benchmarks. Typical floating rate benchmarks are six-month LIBOR, prime, or A1-P1 commercial paper rates from published sources. A typical fixed-rate benchmark is the Treasury yield for an appropriate maturity, plus some markup.

Swap agreements are made on a *trade date,* but the calculation of the interest streams to be swapped does not begin until the swap's *effective date,* which may be one, two, five, or more business days after the trade date. A forward swap can be created by setting the effective date well after the trade date.

The benchmark and any markup thereon are established and observed on the trade date. The fixed rate payment stream for the life of the swap and the first portion of the floating-rate stream are then fixed.

The interest stream on the swap are calculated from the effective date until the first *adjustment date,* a span of time equal to that of the floating-rate benchmark. On the *payment date* of the swap, which typically coincides with the adjustment date, the fixed- and floating-interest payments due are netted and the counterparty owing more pays the difference to the other counterparty. From the first adjustment date to the next, the fixed-rate stream will not vary, but the floating-rate stream will be based on the floating-rate benchmark observed on the first adjustment date. This process repeats until the termination date of the swap, which is the date the fixed-rate benchmark security matures.

Swap Documentation

Counterparties may wish to enter into several swaps with a given dealer over time as their balance sheets change or grow. To minimize the time and expense of creating swap agreements, swap users often enter into a *master swap agreement* which names the counterparties, and sets forth covenants, assumptions, definitions, methods of calculations, etc. When a specific swap is desired, the counterparties sign a supplement to the master agreement, which can be a one- or two-page document setting forth the bare essentials of the swap. Master agreements often incorporate the *ISDA Code of Standard Wording, Assumptions, and Provisions for Swaps,* written by the International Swap Dealers Association, an industry practice group.

Variations in Swap Characteristics

While the large volume of swap agreements has promoted standardization, the swap market is still over-the-counter in nature, and many variations in swap structure appear, for example:

- The fixed-rate benchmark may be quoted on an actual/ 365-day year, but used to make 30/360-day calculations of fixed-rate payments.
- A markup or discount on the floating-rate benchmark may be used.
- Payment dates for the fixed- or floating-interest stream may be mismatched.
- The fixed stream may be calculated on a semiannually compounded basis but paid quarterly. Conversely,the floating-rate stream may be calculated and adjusted quarterly but paid semiannually.
- A counterparty may purchase a put on the swap, enabling him to get out of the swap, if he so elects before the termination date.

With the exception of the last variation, the effect of these different structures on swap cash flows is easily calculated using the rate formulas from Chapter 1 and Appendix 1.

Gauging Swap Cost Effectiveness

Swaps modify the liability cash flow pattern of the counterparties involved and hence change the counterparties' costs of funds. Prospective counterparties must gauge the effect on their cost of funds when considering a swap. The standard measure of a swap's cost is called the *all-in cost* (AIC).

A slightly more precise means of gauging swap costs is to project cash flows for the life of the swap and then calculate the internal rate of return on the swap, treating it as the issuance of a synthetic liability. Either AIC or IRR will allow you to compare swaps to other alternatives which result in the same interest sensitivity.

A third method of analyzing swaps is to compare the swap cost to the cost the U.S. Treasury would incur to create the same liability cash flow pattern. This *spread to Treasury* might allow the prospective counterparty to decide between alternatives with differing interest sensitivity characteristics. The calculation of each of these alternatives is best illustrated by an example, such as the swap described in Table 5-1.

Two complications are associated with this swap. First, the

Table 5-1 A Simple Swap Example

Today's Date: April 27, 1987
Trade Date: April 20, 1987
Effective Date: April 27, 1987
Payment Dates:
    Floating: Every 3 months
    Fixed: Every 6 months
Termination Date: April 27, 1989
Notional Amount: $10,000,000
Floating Benchmark: 3-month LIBOR "flat" − 6⅞%
Fixed Benchmark: 2-year Treasury + 80 basis points, 7.69%
Calculation Method: Straight-line, 365-day
Current fixed rate payor liabilities: 3-month CDs at LIBOR
                                        + 40 basis points

---

fixed-rate payor pays 40 basis points more for his liabilities than he receives from the floating-rate payor; second, the fixed rate payor receives floating-rate payments quarterly but pays fixed-rate payments semiannually.

The all-in cost of the swap to the fixed-rate payor is the fixed rate benchmark plus markup, 7.69%, plus that portion of his short-term liability cost which is not covered by the floating rate payments he receives, 0.40%. The AIC is, therefore, 8.09%.

To calculate the internal rate of return on the swap, the fixed-rate payor must project out the cash flows resulting from the swap: 40 basis points per quarter, or $10,000 of liability cost not covered by the floating-rate payments, and $394,500 of fixed-rate interest payments due every six months. The fixed-rate payor must treat the swap as if he is issuing a new, two-year liability (using the proceeds to retire short-term CDs) and then paying off this liability when it matures in two years (and replacing it with short-term CDs). The hypothetical cash flows from this liability are shown in Table 5-2.

Calculating an internal rate of return on these cash flows, borrowers will find that they are paying 8.01% on a quarterly compounded basis for their synthetic two-year liability. This translates to 8.094 on a semiannually compounded basis, almost the same as the AIC. Borrowers can compare this cost to the cost

Table 5-2 Hypothetical Cash flows
of a Two-Year Liability Swap

Time	Cash flows
Now	+ 10,000,000
3 months	− 10,000
6 months	− 394,500
9 months	− 10,000
12 months	− 394,500
15 months	− 10,000
18 months	− 394,500
21 months	− 10,000
24 months	− 10,394,500

of issuing two-year liabilities, or other alternatives with similar cash flows, to those resulting from the swap.

To determine the spread to Treasury that will be paid by entering the swap, the fixed-rate payor must project out cash flows the same as for calculating an interval rate of return, and must observe or gauge pure discount Treasury yields for quarterly maturities out to two years. By trial and error, he determines a markup over the Treasury yield curve, which will result in the sum of the present values of the swap cash outflows being equal to the notional amount of the swap, as illustrated in Table 5-3.

The fixed-rate payor can perform a similar analysis on alternatives to the swap and can make comparisons of the spread to Treasury even between alternatives with differing cash flow patterns. The object, of course, is to identify the alternative which costs as close to Treasury rates as possible.

Swap Interest Sensitivity

The analysis of spread to Treasury in Table 5-3 is easily extended to determine the basis point value and slope point value of the synthetic liability created by the swap. By adding one basis point to the markup over Treasury yields and seeing how the present value of cash flows changes, we can measure the swap's basis point value as in Table 5-4.

By adding one basis point per year until payment of a cash

Table 5-3 Analysis of a Spread to Treasury Swap

Time	Pure Discount Treasury Rates*	Markup (Spread to Treasury)	Swap Cash Outflows	Present Value of Swap Cash Outflows, Using Treasury Rate Plus Markup
3 mo.	5.74	1.01205	10,000	9,835
6 mo.	6.30	1.01205	394,500	380,586
9 mo.	6.40	1.01205	10,000	9,469
12 mo.	6.50	1.01205	394,500	366,455
15 mo.	6.69	1.01205	10,000	9,098
18 mo.	6.85	1.01205	394,500	351,407
21 mo.	6.99	1.01205	10,000	8,717
24 mo.	7.11	1.01205	10,394,500	8,864,438
				10,000,005

*semiannually compounded

flow to the appropriate Treasury rate plus markup, we can measure the effect of a steepening in the Treasury curve on the present value of swap cash outflows, i.e. the swap's slope point value. This is illustrated in Table 5-5.

Table 5-4 Measuring the Basis Point Value of a Swap

Time	Pure Discount Treasury Rates	Markup 1.01205 + 1BPV	Swap Cash Outflows	Present Value of Swap Cash Outflows
3 mo.	5.74	1.01305	10,000	9,835
6 mo.	6.30	1.01305	394,500	380,567
9 mo.	6.40	1.01305	10,000	9,468
12 mo.	6.50	1.01305	394,500	366,419
15 mo.	6.69	1.01305	10,000	9,098
18 mo.	6.85	1.01305	394,500	351,357
21 mo.	6.99	1.01305	10,000	8,716
24 mo.	7.11	1.01305	10,394,500	8,862,734
				9,998,194

BPV = 10,000,0005 − 9,998,194 = 1,811

Table 5-5 Measuring the Slope Point Value of a Swap

Time	Pure Discount Treasury Rates	Markup 1.01205 + 1 BP/year	Swap Cash Outflows	Present Value of Swap Cash Outflows
3 mo.	5.74	5.743	10,000	9,835
6 mo.	6.30	6.305	394,500	380,576
9 mo.	6.40	6.408	10,000	9,468
12 mo.	6.50	6.510	394,500	366,419
15 mo.	6.69	6.913	10,000	9,074
18 mo.	6.85	6.865	394,500	351,331
21 mo.	6.99	7.008	10,000	8,747
24 mo.	7.11	7.130	10,394,500	8,861,031
				9,996,451

SPV = 10,000,0005 − 9,996,451 = 3,555

Limitations and Risks of Swaps

Swaps are best used as a long-term solution to long-term mismatches between asset and liability interest sensitivity. The swap market is fairly liquid; nonetheless, the transaction costs and large minimum size required to do swaps efficiently make them less suitable as a means of controlling transient or fluctuating rate risk. Thus futures or options are the more appropriate tool for temporary hedges or for controlling financial product origination conduit risk.

The most often cited risk of swaps is the risk of defaults, when one counterparty reneges on his agreement to make fixed or floating payments. Swap dealers argue that their large capital bases makes dealer-originated swaps less susceptible to default; however, the size of dealer swap books can become quite large relative to their capital, and, on occasion, can be deliberately mismatched as a speculative play on rate changes. Still, defaults to date have been extremely rare.

A second risk associated with swaps which is seldom discussed rests principally with the fixed-rate payor. In evaluating a swap, the fixed-rate payor assumes that he can continue to issue short-term liabilities at a stable markup over the floating-rate benchmark. If he loses that ability during the life of the swap—

perhaps due to deteriorating credit quality—he may find that the floating-rate payments received do not nearly cover the liability costs. Had the fixed-rate payor issued fixed-term liabilities rather than swapping, he would not force this risk. In evaluating the attractiveness of swaps, the fixed-rate payor needs to gauge the cost of self-insuring his ability to issue short-term debt.

Conclusion

Swaps are often the risk management tool of choice in the face of large, long-term rate risk exposures. Their use can often reduce transaction costs and control basic risk better than other alternatives.

Swaps control the same types of risks as futures do and can be evaluated using the concepts and tools developed in earlier chapters. A different kind of risk is encountered when an asset or liability confers the right—but not the obligation—to receive or pay a given set of cash flows. Futures and swaps cannot control such risks as well as a third tool—the *option*. We shall explore the nature of options in Chapter 6.

CHAPTER 6

Option Concepts

Important developments in the theory of option price behavior have changed, to a remarkable extent, the ways investors analyze and hedge investments. A better understanding of option behavior has made investors aware of option features embedded in many common fixed income securities. The rise of liquid option markets has given investors new ways to manage their risk exposure.

This chapter is intended to develop a basic understanding of option price behavior and of the mathematical formulas used to evaluate and predict option prices. The first half of the chapter describes informal ways to look at option prices which will give readers a correct intuitive feel for option behavior. The second half of the chapter describes the most often discussed option pricing model and its use and shows how options pricing model arises from intuitively understandable arbitrage arguments and assumptions.

Option Features and Terminology

Options have a variety of special features and a jargon which is used to describe them. An option is the right (not the obligation) to buy or sell a specific underlying security at an agreed on price on or up until a specified date in the future. At any given time this underlying security has a market value called its *underlying price.*

An option to buy a security is deemed a *call option* or *call;* the call owner has the right to call the underlying security from the call seller. The option to sell a security is deemed a *put option* or *put;* the put owner has the right to put the underlying security to the put seller. Sellers of options are often called *option writers;* to write an option is to sell it.

An option always specifies the price at which the underlying security may be called or put, the *strike* or *exercise price*. Note that the strike price of an option does not vary over time, while the underlying price in all likelihood does.

Options have a lifespan which terminates on an agreed on *expiration date*. An option which can be exercised only on the expiration date is called an *European option*, while an option which can be exercised on any day up until expiration is called an *American option*.

These terms are misnomers, since most exchange-traded options in Europe and America are American options. However, most theoretical models of option pricing are based on European options. Fortunately, the two behave similarly in many respects, and European option theory is readily extended to American options.

Options are assets to their owner and liabilities to their writers. They are bought and sold at a price or option premium.

Even an option which is not traded on an exchange, but is part of another security, has an implicit premium associated with it. Understanding how this option premium behaves is prerequisite to understanding the price behavior of securities with option features.

Option Price Behavior

An option's premium consists of two parts—an *intrinsic value* component and a *time value* component. Intrinsic value is the easier of the two to understand. Suppose a charity is given an option at no cost. The option's intrinsic value is the profit they could realize by exercising the option. This profit is a function of the option's strike price and the underlying security's price.

In the case of a call, if the underlying security price is higher than the strike price, the charity could exercise the call, buying the security at the strike price, and immediately resell the security at the market price. Their profit would be the difference between the underlying security price and the strike price, but in no event less than zero, since they could always let the option expire unexercised.

In the case of a put, if the underlying security price is lower than the strike price, the charity could buy the underlying security and exercise the put, effectively reselling the security at the strike price. Their profit would be the difference between the strike price and the underlying security price, but never less than zero, since they could always let the option expire unexercised.

The relationship between intrinsic value and underlying security price is shown in Figure 6-1.

We can summarize Figure 6-1 as follows:

Intrinsic value is the profit made by exercising an option, ignoring the initial premium paid.

For a call, intrinsic value is the greater of (Underlying Price − Strike) or zero.

For a put, intrinsic value is the greater of (Strike − Underlying Price) or zero.

An option with a positive intrinsic value is said to be *in-the-money*. When an option's strike price exactly equals the underlying security price, it is said to be *at-the-money*. If the option's intrinsic value is zero and it is not at-the-money, it is said to be *out-of-the-money*. The premium demanded by rational option writers will never be less than intrinsic value for American options, and, in the case of European options, never less than the present value of profit from exercise on the expiration date.

Notice the asymmetrical shape of the intrinsic value functions graphed in Figure 6-1. Intrinsic value can rise an unlimited amount in calls (or until the underlying security is worthless in puts) but has a minimum value of zero. It is this asymmetry that gives options their unique risk properties.

Time Value

One who reads listed option prices in the newspaper will note that options sell at a nonzero price even when they are out-of-the-money, i.e., even though their intrinsic value is zero. The

Figure 6-1 The Relationship Between Intrinsic Value and Underlying
Security Price

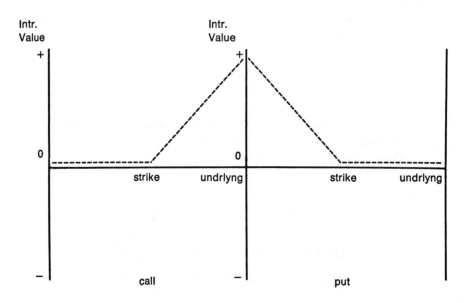

amount by which an option's total premium exceeds its intrinsic value is called *time value*. Time value is the amount the most eager buyers of options are willing to pay for the possibility that an option's intrinsic value may increase before expiration. The odds that an option's intrinsic value will increase (and hence the time premium rational option buyers are willing to pay) are influenced by three factors: (1) the time remaining to expiration, (2) the volatility of the underlying security's price, and (3) the nearness of the underlying security's price to the strike price of the option.

If the underlying security's price has a steady volatility over time, it is likelier to wander above a call's strike price in six months than in two weeks. Thus, a call buyer would be willing to pay more for a call with six months to expiration then a call two weeks to expiration, all other factors being equal. Time value is greater, the more time to expiration. This effect is illustrated in Figure 6-2.

Figure 6-3 illustrates why the larger the volatility of the underlying security's price the greater the odds that an option's intrinsic value will increase. The high volatility of the underlying security price in Figure 6-3a suggests that it would not require unusual behavior of the underlying security's price to move the depicted call into-the-money. In contrast, the underlying security price's behavior in Figure 6-3b would have to change markedly to move the call into-the-money to rise above the strike price before expiration. Thus, more time value would be paid for the call in 6-3a than for the call in 6-3b.

Intuitively, many people conclude that time value rises as an option goes further and further into-the-money. In reality, the odds that an option's intrinsic value will increase further, and thus its time value, reaches a maximum when an option is just at-the-money. Consider a call with three months to expiration and a given price volatility. If the option is out-of-the-money, a move

Figure 6-2 Comparison of the Time Value of a Security

a. Two months to expiration   **b. Six months to expiration**

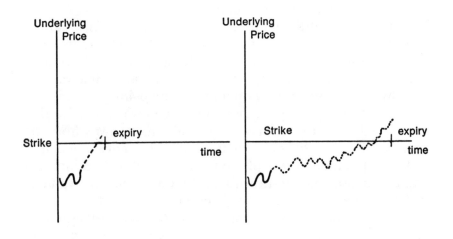

Figure 6-3 The Intrinsic Value of an Option Relative to the Volatility of its Underlying Price

a. High Volatility   b. Low Volatility

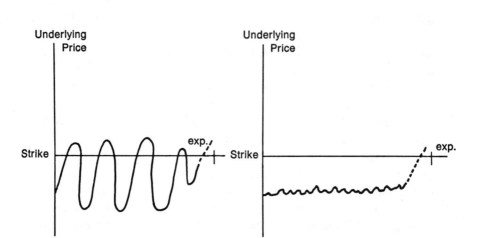

further out-of-the-money cannot hurt intrinsic value, which remains at zero. However, a move *toward-the-money* will not raise intrinsic value unless that move is large enough to put the call in-the-money (Figure 6-4a). An option buyer will pay some, but not a lot of time value for this option.

If the call is at-the-money, a move out-of-the-money cannot hurt intrinsic value, but any move into-the-money, however small, will increase intrinsic value. Because time and volatility cannot diminish, but only increase intrinsic value, time value is very high for at-the-money options (Figure 6-4b).

If the call is deep in-the-money, a move further in-the-money will increase intrinsic value, but a move away from the money will hurt intrinsic value until the price moves enough to put the option at- or out-of-the-money. Because volatility is a two-edged sword for in-the-money options, their time value is not as high as for at-the-money options (Figure 6-4c).

Time value, then, is low when an option is out-of-the-money, rises to its maximum level when the option is at-the-money, and

Figure 6-4 The Effort of Time Value on an Option's Intrinsic Value

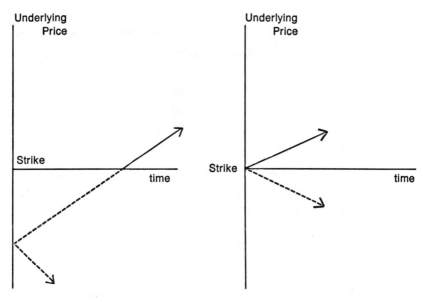

a. Toward-the-money

b. At-the-money

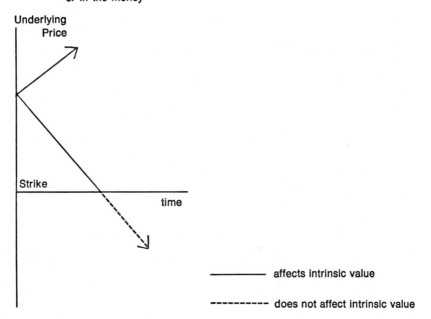

c. In-the-money

——— affects intrinsic value

---------- does not affect intrinsic value

then declines as the option moves into-the-money as in Figure 6-5.

We can summarize Figure 6-5, as follows:

Time value is the worth of an option over and above the option's intrinsic value. Time value reflects the odds that intrinsic value will increase before expiration.

Time value is higher
1) the longer the time to expiration;
2) the longer the volatility of the underlying security price; and
3) the closer the option is to being at-the-money.

Total option premium is the sum of intrinsic value plus time value.

Summing an option's intrinsic and time values, we can infer what an option's total premium should be for a given underlying security price. This is illustrated in Figure 6-6.

Figure 6-5 Time Value as a Function of Underlying Price

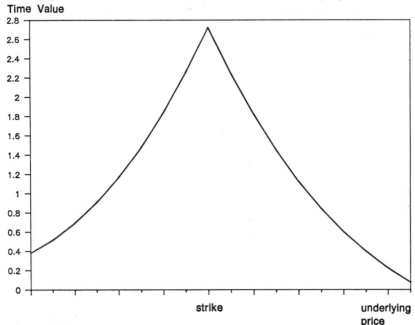

Figure 6-6 Total Call Premium as the Sum of Intrinsic and Time Value

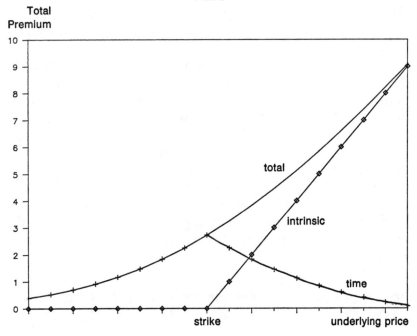

Option Price Sensitivity

Once we know what an option's price should be, given the underlying security's price, we can deduce what change in option premium will result from a given change in the underlying security's price. This change is called the option's *delta* and can be defined informally as follows:

An option's delta is the number of cents by which the option's premium changes, when the underlying security changes in price by a dollar.

Geometrically, delta is the slope of the total option premium line in Figure 6-6. Although we have not yet acquired the tools necessary to quantify delta precisely, we can develop some rules of thumb to gauge the approximate delta of an option for a given underlying security price as follows: (1) delta is near zero for a deep out-of-the-money option; (2) it is near .5 at-the-money; and (3) approaches one for a deep in-the-money option. Delta is a negative number for puts and a positive number for calls. It is shown in Figure 6-7.

This sharpness of the delta graph is a function of the richness of the time value of the option. If there is a long time to expiration, or if there is high volatility of the underlying security price, time premium is rich for every level of the underlying security's price, and the delta function is gradual. If there is little volatility or time to expiration, the delta function looks like a step, staying very close to zero when the option is out-of-the-money, then quickly shooting toward one (or minus one for puts) when the option is in-the-money. The sharpness of the delta curve can be measured by observing how its slope changes as the underlying price changes. This measure is called the option's *gamma*.

An option's gamma is the change in the delta which occurs when the underlying security's price changes by a dollar.

Gamma is low when an option is in- or out-of-the-money, and high when the option is at-the-money. The sharper the shape of the delta function, the higher gamma will be for an at-the-money option, and the lower it will be for away-from-the-money options, as is illustrated in Figure 6-8.

Consider an option on a fixed-income security. What is the option's basis point value? Using the techniques introduced in Chapter 1, the *BPV* of the underlying security can be measured. Knowing the delta of the option, the *BPV* of the option is easy to obtain:

$$BPV_{option} = BPV_{underlying} \times Delta_{option}. \qquad (6\text{-}1)$$

Because delta varies with the price of an underlying security, the *BPV* of an option is less stable than that of the underlying security. To determine the change in an option's BPV which results from a $1 change in the underlying price, multiply the option's BPV by its gamma.

Figure 6-7 Option Delta

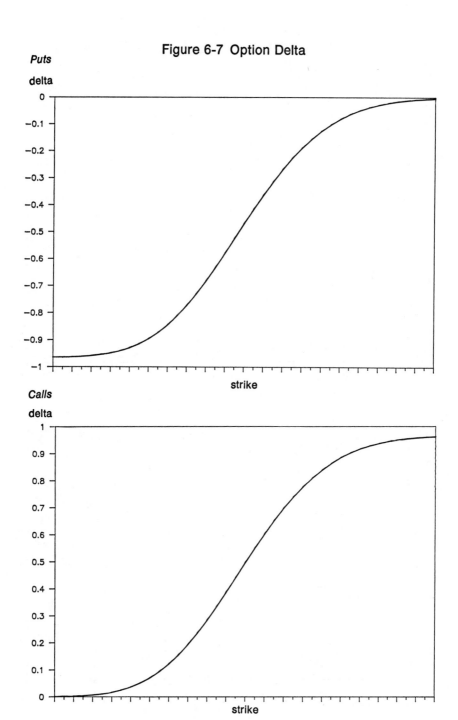

Puts

delta

Calls

delta

Figure 6-8 Option Delta and Gamma

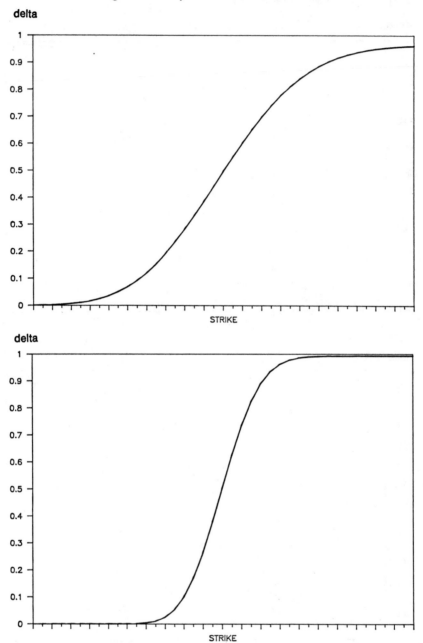

gamma

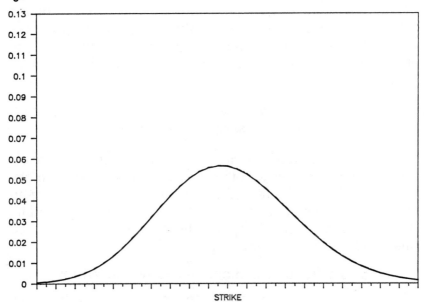

STRIKE

gamma

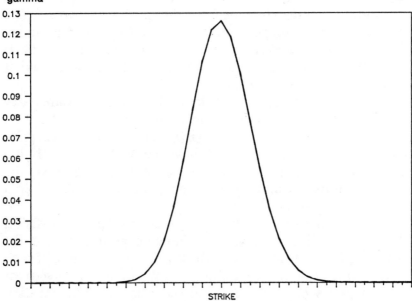

STRIKE

Option Theta

An option's time value is high when there is a long time to expiration, and low when expiration is close at hand. It follows that, all other factors being equal, the time value of a given option will decline as time passes and will reach zero at expiration. The rate at which this time decay occurs is called the option's *theta*.

An option's theta is the change in option premium which results from the passage of a given unit of time.

Theta is relatively low when an option has a long time to expiration, but increases with the passage of time, when each day represents a larger fraction of the option's remaining life. For an at-the-money option, theta increases steadily until expiration. For away-from-the money options, theta increases to a point and then declines shortly before expiration.

Short Option Positions and Covered Writes

Until now we have looked at options exclusively from the perspective of the owner of a single option. We should expand our understanding to include the position of option writers. The values of short option positions are shown in Figures 6-9a and 6-9b. Option writers receive premium for the options they write. If the options expire out-of-the-money or at-the-money, a writer keeps the premium received.

However, if the options expire in-the-money, they are likely to be exercised. In the case of a call, this means that the option writer will have to buy the underlying security at the market price and deliver it at a loss to the call buyer at the strike price. In the case of a put, it means that the put writer will have to pay the strike price for an underlying security, the worth of which is lower than the strike.

Often owners of an underlying security will write calls on the security, with the goal of enhancing returns should the security fail to rally above the call strike price. The value of such *covered write* positions (excluding option premium received) for various prices of the underlying securities are illustrated in Figure 6-10.

Figure 6-9 Short Option Position Values

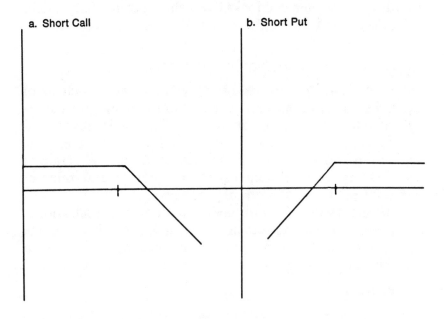

a. Short Call

b. Short Put

Figure 6-10 Covered Call Writing

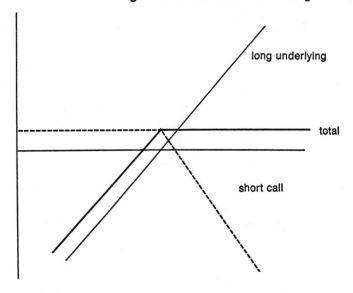

long underlying

total

short call

The total value function of a long position in the underlying security and a written call looks like a short-put position and, in fact, behaves very much like a short in-the-money put.

Quantifying Option Concepts

Option evaluation procedures have been developed which are in widespread use in the financial community. These procedures are difficult to understand intuitively. They make several assumptions which in practice may be violated, and, therefore, yield results which can be misinterpreted. Taken with a grain of salt, these procedures nonetheless constitute useful rules of thumb for predicting option price behavior.

The most widely known model of option price behavior is the Black-Scholes model, developed in the 1970s by Fisher Black and Myron Scholes. As modified for application to options on fixed income securities and futures, the model is as follows:

Call Premium (6-2)

$$C = e^{-r \times t}[U \times e^{(h \times t)} \times N(d_1) - S \times N(d_2)]$$

Put Premium (6-3)

$$P = e^{-r \times t}[U \times e^{(h \times t)} \times (N(d_1) - 1) - S \times (N(d_2) - 1)]$$

In the above,

$$d_1 = [\ln (U \times e^{(h \times t)}/S) + .5 \times V^2 \times t]/(v \times t^{.5})$$
$$d_2 = d_1 - V \times t^{.5}$$

Call Delta (6-4)

$$Delta_c = e^{(h-r) \times t} \times N(d_1)$$

Put Delta (6-5)

$$Delta_P = e^{(h-r) \times t} \times (N(d_1) - 1)$$

Put, Call Gamma (6-6)

$$Gamma = \frac{N'(d_1)}{U \times V \times t^{.5}}$$

(same for puts and calls with same U, S, V, r, t)

Put Theta   (6-7)

$$Theta_p = e^{-rt} \times \left\{ \frac{U}{2 \times t^{.5}} \times N(d_1) + S \times e^{ht} \times (h - r) \right.$$
$$\left. \times [N(d_1) - 1] + S \times r \times [N(d_2) - 1] \right\}$$

Call Theta   (6-8)

$$Theta_c = e^{-rt} \times \left[\frac{U}{2 \times t^{.5}} \times N(d_1) + S \times e^{ht} \times (h - r) \times N(d_1) \right.$$
$$\left. + S \times r \times N(d_2) \right]$$

where

C = call premium

P = put premium

r = short term rate, continuously compounded

t = time to expiration in years

h = rate for cost of carry (for securities, h equals $r - y$ where y equals security yield; h equals zero for futures)

U = underlying security

S = strike price

V = volatility [standard deviation of log of proportional underlying security price changes $- \ln (U_T/U_{T-1})$]

$N(x)$ = the standard normal distribution function of (x)

$N'(x) = (1/[2\pi]^{.5}) \times e(x^2/2)$

The model assumes the following: (1) changes in the price of the security underlying an option are lognormally distributed; (2) the volatility of the underlying security price is constant over time; (3) when the underlying security price changes, it does so by frequent tiny changes, rather than in large jumps; and (4) traders incur no transactions costs; and (5) the short-term interest rate is constant. Other technical assumptions are implicit in the derivation of the model.

In practice, of course, underlying security prices may go through quiet or turbulent periods; short-term rates fluctuate; and security prices may jump by large amounts between trading sessions or in a short period of time. An underlying fixed income security's duration, and hence price volatility, may shrink due to the passage of time. An option's premium may move by more or less than predicted from the delta calculated via the Black-Scholes model if any of the model's assumptions are violated.

Getting Volatility and the Normal Distribution Function

Two formidable deterrents to using the Black-Scholes formula in practical applications exist. They are the variable v (or *volatility*) and the variables $N(d_1)$ and $N(d_2)$ which appear in the Black-Scholes formula.

Volatility can be thought of as a measure of the size of typical changes in the price of the underlying security. Two methods are used to obtain volatility measures in practice. One is to measure the standard deviation of continuously compounded percentage price changes over some period of time. To measure historical volatility, obtain a price history; for example, daily closing prices for the last n days. Determine the continuously compounded daily return for each day, $\ln (U_t/U_{t-1})$, where U_t equals the underlying security price on day t, U_{t-1} equals the underlying security price for the previous day, and $\ln (x)$ is the natural log of a given number x. Next, calculate the mean daily return:

$$\text{mdr} = \sum_{t=2}^{n} \ln (U_t/U_{t-1})/(n - 1). \qquad (6\text{-}9a)$$

Notice that there are n daily prices in the history but only $n - 1$ daily returns. Calculate the variance of daily returns and annualize it by multiplying by the number of return observations which occur in a year. The square root of this is the volatility used in the Black-Scholes formula:

$$V = \sqrt{\frac{\sum_{t=2}^{n} [\ln (U_t/U_{t-1}) - \text{mdr}]^2}{n - 2}} \times \text{obs. per year.} \qquad (6\text{-}9b)$$

The above formula represents the annualized standard deviation of continuously compounded returns.

When daily returns are used to calculated volatility, observations per year in formula 6-9b is sometimes set to 365 (the number of days in a calendar year), but is more often is set to 260 to reflect the fact that trading only occurs on the five business days of each week.

Another approach to measuring volatility involves no gathering of historical data but rather an assumption that the market fairly prices options. In this approach, C or P, U, r, t, and S are plugged into the Black-Scholes formula, and a value for v is chosen which makes the resulting equation true. V is chosen via iterative guesses.

The second major hurdle to using the Black-Scholes formula is in determining $N(d_1)$ and $N(d_2)$. What $N(x)$, the normal distribution function, does is to calculate the probability that an observation, drawn from a normally distributed sample of observations, will have a value equal to or greater than x. In the context of the Black-Scholes formula, you might think of it as a way to measure the odds that an option will finish in-the-money. Here is a formula that will give you a close approximation of $N(x)$:

$$N(x) = 1 - 1/\sqrt{2\pi} \times e^{-(x^2/2)} \times (b_1 \times k + b_2 \times k^2 + b_3 \times k^3$$
$$+ b_4 \times k^4 + b_5 \times k^5) \qquad \text{(6-10a)}$$

where
π = 3.141592654, a constant
$k = 1/(1 + a \times x)$
$a = .2316419$
$b_1 = .319381530$
$b_2 = -.356563782$
$b_3 = 1.781477937$
$b_4 = -1.821255978$
$b_5 = 1.330274429$

Source: Cox & Rubenstein, *Options Markets*

If x is a negative number, substitute its absolute value in the above formula and subtract the result from one, i.e:

$$N(-x) = 1 - N(x). \qquad \text{(6-10b)}$$

Understanding the Option Models

The Black-Scholes and related models are difficult to grasp on an intuitive level. Nonetheless, the common-sense roots of the model are discernable using intuitively appealing concepts and a good deal of mental effort.

We will begin with some simple arbitrage arguments. Next we will add some assumptions about the likely expiration price of the underlying security and about risk preferences in the option markets. This will enable us to arrive at a model which is the mechanical equivalent of the Black-Scholes model. Finally, we will see how the Black-Scholes model can be derived without making any assumptions about the risk-preferences of option market participants.

Variable Definitions

A host of new variables must be introduced to discuss option pricing in detail. For ease of reference, the names we will use for these variables are detailed below:

C = Total price or premium of a call

C_h = Call premium if the underlying price = U_h

C_1 = Call premium if the underlying price = U_1

P = Total price of a put

U_n = Price of the underlying security today

U_x = Price of the underlying security at expiration

U_h = High price which the underlying security might have at a given point in time

U_1 = Low price which the underlying security might have at a given point in time

S = Strike price of a put or call

r = Rate of interest, continuously compounded

t = Time to expiration

p_{U_x} = Probability that a price U_x will prevail at expiration

B = An amount borrowed

X = A quantity of calls bought or sold

Arbitrage Constraints on Option Prices

The first arbitrage argument to consider is a trivial one, which demonstrates that puts and calls can never be worth less than zero: If arbitragers were paid to buy puts or calls, they could let the options expire worthless and keep the amount they were paid to buy them. Thus:

$$P \geqslant 0 \qquad (6\text{-}11)$$

$$C \geqslant 0 \qquad (6\text{-}12)$$

must hold true.

A second arbitrage strategy will ensure that, given U_n, S, r, t, and P, the price of a call will be known with certainty. Consider a call with a known market price:

| | | At Expiration | | | |
| Now | | $U_x \geqslant S$ | | $U_x < S$ | |
Action	Cashflow	Action	Cashflow	Action	Cashflow
Buy Call	$-C$	Exercise call	$-S$	Call expires	0
Sell Put	$+P$	Put expires	0	Put exercised	$-S$
Short underlying security	$+U_n$	Cover short	0	Cover short	0
Lend	$-Se^{-rt}$	Loan repaid	S	Loan repaid	S
Net CF: $P+U_n-C-Se^{-rt}$			0		0

By buying the call, selling the put, short-selling the underlying security, and lending the present value of the strike price, arbitragers can ensure that their net cash flow at expiration will be zero no matter what. Therefore, if $P + U_n - C - Se^{-rt} > 0$, the arbitragers will do the trade and receive a profit with no risk. Conversely, if $P + U_n - C - Se^{-rt} < 0$, the arbitragers will do the opposite trade, again locking in a profit with no risk. Therefore, $P + U_n - C - Se^{-rt} = 0$ if arbitrage is to be precluded.

We can rearrange the above, as follows:

$$P = Se^{-rt} - U_n + C \qquad (6\text{-}13)$$

$$C = U_n - Se^{-rt} + P. \qquad (6\text{-}14)$$

This relationship is called *put/call parity*.

A third arbitrage argument establishes a minimum price of a put or call, given r, t, S, and U_n. Consider this arbitrage using a call:

	Now	At Expiration $U_x \geqslant S$		At Expiration $U_x < S$	
Action	Cashflow	Action	Cashflow	Action	Cashflow
Buy Call	$-C$	Exercise call	$-S$	Call expires Buy underlying security	0 $-U_x$
Short underlying security	$+U_n$	Cover short	0	Cover short	0
Lend	$-Se^{-n}$	Loan repaid	S	Loan repaid	S
Net CF:	$U_n - Se^{-n} - C$		0		$S - U_n$ $(S - U_n > 0)$

By doing the trade, the arbitrageur ensures himself a non-negative cash flow at expiration. Thus, to prevent arbitrage:

$$C > U_n - Se^{-rt} \qquad (6\text{-}15)$$

Notice that the arbitrager could not do the reverse of this trade without risk if C were greater than $U_n - Se^{-n}$.

A similar arbitrage can be done in puts:

	Now	At Expiration $U_x \geqslant S$		At Expiration $U_x < S$	
Buy Put	$-P$	Put expires	0	Exercise Put	S
Buy underlying security	$-U_n$	Sell underlying security	U_x		
Borrow	Se^{-n}	Repay Loan	S	Repay Loan	$-S$
	$Se^{-n} - U_n - P$		$U_x - S$ $(U_x - S > 0)$		0

Thus, at a minimum,

$$P > Se^{-rt} - U_n. \qquad (6\text{-}16)$$

Uncertain Underlying Price at Expiration

The minima defined in Equations 6-11 through 6-16 allow us to determine an exact market value in a call or put only in one case, where the price of the underlying security at expiration is known with certainty.

The relationships described so far thus provide an incomplete picture of option value if there is uncertainty about the underlying security price at expiration. Consider an example:

S = Put, Call, Strike: $10

t = Time to expiration: 1 year

r = 1 year term rate: .10

U_n = Underlying price now: $10

U_x = Underlying price at expiration

Possible Values of U_x

$ 5	20% probability
$15	50% probability
$25	30% probability

No other values of U_x are possible.

Let us first evaluate the call using the constraints discussed so far. At minimum, the call price equals zero. The call price is also greater than or equal to:

$$C \geqslant U_n - Se^{-rt}$$
$$C \geqslant 10 - 10e^{-.1}$$
$$C \geqslant .95.$$

The put price is worth at least zero. The put price is also worth at least:

$$P \geqslant Se^{-rt} - U_n$$
$$P \geqslant 9.0484 - 10$$
$$P \geqslant -.95.$$

Thus the put can only be worth zero for certain so far. Put/call parity tells us that, given the call price, the put must be worth

$$P = Se^{-rt} - U_n + C$$
$$P = 9.05 - 10 + .95$$
$$P = 0.$$

By put/call parity, the put would be worth nothing as well, if the call were worth $.95. Yet, if the put costs nothing, an arbitrage is possible:

		At Expiration			
Now		$U_x \geqslant S$		$U_x < S$	
Action	Cashflow	Action	Cashflow	Action	Cashflow
Buy put	0	Puts expire	0	Buy underlying security	−5
				Exercise put	10
					5

There is a 20% probability that the puts will be exercisable at expiration for a $5 profit. By the same token, there is a significant probability that the call will be worth more than implied by Equation 6-15:

Now $U_n = 10$		At Expiration			
		$U_x \geqslant S$		$U_x < S$	
Action	Cashflow	Action	Cashflow	Action	Cashflow
Buy Call	−.95	Exercise call	−10	Call expires	0
Short underlying				Buy underlying	
security	+10			security	−5
		Cover short	0	Cover short	0
Lend	9.05	Repayment	10	Repayment	10
	0		0		5

There is again a 20% probability that a net zero investment now will result in a $5 profit at expiration if the call price is $.95.

An individual who is *risk neutral*—defined as one who seeks to maximize expected wealth and is indifferent to the degree of uncertainty concerning the expected payoff of an investment— would be willing to pay a calculable amount more to own the put or call. In the case of the call, if $U_n - Se^{-rt} = 0$, the buyer would be willing to pay the present value of expected payoff at expiration:

$$C_1 = e^{-rt} \times \sum_{U_x=S}^{\infty} p_{U_x} \times (U_x - S). \qquad (6\text{-}17a)$$

If $U_n - Se^{-rt} > 0$, the call buyer would buy the call, short the underlying security and lend the net cash inflow. He or she would be willing to pay for the calls:

$$C_2 = U_n - Se^{-rt} + \sum_{U_x=0}^{S} p_{U_x}(S - U_x) \times e^{-rt} \qquad (6\text{-}17b)$$

In the case of the put, if $Se^{-rt} - U_n = 0$, the buyer must be willing to pay

$$P_1 = e^{-rt} \times \sum_{U_x=0}^{S} p_{U_x} \times (S - U_x). \qquad (6\text{-}18a)$$

If $Se^{-rt} - U_n > 0$, the buyer must be willing to pay

$$P_2 = Se^{-rt} - U_n + \sum_{U_x=S}^{\infty} p_{U_x} \times (U_x - S) \times e^{-rt}. \qquad (6\text{-}18b)$$

The fair price of the calls and puts must equal

$$C = \max [C_1, C_2], \qquad (6\text{-}17c)$$

and

$$P = \max [P_1, P_2]. \qquad (6\text{-}18c)$$

In any event, put/call parity must hold true:

$$P = Se^{-rt} - U_n + C$$
$$C = U_n - Se^{-rt} + P.$$

Applying Equations 6-17 and 6-18 to the preceding example,

$C_1 = e^{-.1} \times [.50 \times (15 - 10) + .30 \times (25 - 10)] = 6.33$
$C_2 = 10 - 10 \times e^{-.1} + [.2 \times (10 - 5)] \times e^{-.1} = 1.86$

$C = \max [C_1, C_2] = 6.33$

$P_1 = e^{-.1} \times [.2 \times (10 - 5)]$

$\quad = .90$

$P_2 = 10 \times e^{-.1} - 10 + [.50 \times (15 - 10) + .30 \times (25 - 10) \times e^{-.1}$

$\quad = 5.38.$

$P = \max [P_1, P_2] = 5.38$

Notice that put/call parity holds true:

$$C = 10 - 10 \times e^{-.1} + 5.38 = 6.33$$
$$P = 10 \times e^{-.1} - 10 + 6.33 = 5.38.$$

From a Simple Arbitrage Model to Black-Scholes

By assuming risk neutrality on the part of option market participants, and by making an assumption about the distribution of possible underlying prices at expiration, we can arrive at an option pricing model which is mechanically similar to the Black-Scholes model.

Concerning underlying prices at expiration, we must assume the distribution of probabilities that the underlying security will have a given price at expiration is log-normal, as illustrated in Figure 6-11.

If we were able to graph the probabilities as a function of the natural logarithm of the underlying price at expiration, the resulting curve would become the familiar normal curve used widely in statistics.

Consider another example, in which the underlying prices possible at expiration have an approximately log-normal distribution:

$$S - \text{Put, Call strike} = \$10$$

$$U_n - \text{Underlying price} = \$10$$

$$r - \text{term rate to expiration} = .10$$

$$t - \text{time to expiration} = 1 \text{ year}$$

The probabilities on various underlying prices at expiration are presented in Table 6-1 and Figure 6-12.

Figure 6-11 Log-Normal Probability Distribution

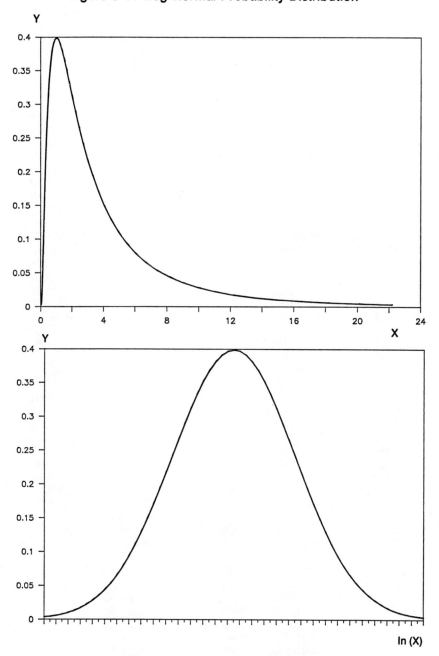

Table 6-1 Probability on Various Underlying Prices at Expiry

Possible Log of U_x	(U_x/U_n)	Probability of U_x	Present Value Expected Exercise Profit (Call)	Present Value Expected Exercise Profit (Put)
1.294081	−0.00122	0.06%		0.004726
1.386961	−0.00138	0.07%		0.005455
1.486508	−0.00171	0.09%		0.006932
1.593200	−0.00220	0.12%		0.009128
1.707550	−0.00265	0.15%		0.011254
1.830107	−0.00339	0.20%		0.014784
1.961460	−0.00407	0.25%		0.018183
2.102241	−0.00499	0.32%		0.022867
2.253126	−0.00596	0.40%		0.028038
2.414840	−0.00696	0.49%		0.033630
2.588162	−0.00797	0.59%		0.039568
2.773923	−0.00923	0.72%		0.047076
2.973017	−0.01055	0.87%		0.055317
3.186401	−0.01166	1.02%		0.062885
3.415100	−0.01289	1.20%		0.071499
3.660214	−0.01407	1.40%		0.080310
3.922920	−0.01497	1.60%		0.087980
4.204482	−0.01585	1.83%		0.095965
4.506252	−0.01642	2.06%		0.102401
4.829681	−0.01673	2.30%		0.107600
5.176324	−0.01672	2.54%		0.110861
5.547847	−0.01637	2.78%		0.111991
5.946035	−0.01564	3.01%		0.110412
6.372803	−0.01455	3.23%		0.106009
6.830201	−0.01303	3.42%		0.098090
7.320428	−0.01126	3.61%		0.087527
7.845840	−0.00909	3.75%		0.073093
8.408964	−0.00668	3.86%		0.055569
9.012504	−0.00410	3.95%		0.035294
9.659363	−0.00137	3.98%		0.012267
10.35264	0.001379	3.98%	0.012699	
11.09569	0.004106	3.95%	0.039161	
11.89207	0.006688	3.86%	0.066083	
12.74560	0.009097	3.75%	0.093162	
13.66040	0.011260	3.61%	0.119565	
14.64085	0.013038	3.42%	0.143613	
15.69168	0.014552	3.23%	0.166346	
16. 81792	0.015647	3.01%	0.185690	
18.02500	0.016379	2.78%	0.201864	
19.31872	0.016725	2.54%	0.214171	
20.70529	0.016739	2.30%	0.222790	
22.19138	0.016420	2.06%	0.227243	

Table 6-1 (*Continued*)

Possible Log of U_x	(U_x/U_n)	Probability of U_x	Present Value Expected Exercise Profit (Call)	Present Value Expected Exercise Profit (Put)
23.78414	0.015855	1.83%	0.228245	
25.49121	0.014971	1.60%	0.224272	
27.32080	0.014070	1.40%	0.219415	
29.28171	0.012892	1.20%	0.209361	
31.38336	0.011665	1.02%	0.197354	
33.63585	0.010553	0.87%	0.186063	
36.05001	0.009232	0.72%	0.169711	
38.63745	0.007974	0.59%	0.152882	
41.41059	0.006962	0.49%	0.139265	
44.38277	0.005961	0.40%	0.124443	
47.56828	0.004990	0.32%	0.108778	
50.98242	0.004072	0.25%	0.092706	
54.64161	0.003396	0.20%	0.080786	
58.56342	0.002651	0.15%	0.065913	
62.76672	0.002204	0.12%	0.057294	
67.27171	0.001715	0.09%	0.046639	
72.10003	0.001382	0.07%	0.039333	
77.27490	0.001226	0.06%	0.036523	

| | | | Call: | 4.071382 | |
| "Volatility":   106.28% (Standard Deviation of Log of U_x/U_n) | | | Put: | | 1.706726 |

Employing Equations 6-17 and 6-18 and the probabilities from Table 6-1, we estimate that $P = \$3.12$ and $C = \$4.07$. These values are identical to those obtained using the Black-Scholes formula, setting V to 119.5%. Notice, however, that this value of V is different from the 106.28% displayed in Table 6-1. The difference results from the fact that the probabilities in Table 6-1 are only an approximation of a log-normal curve.

In fact, with a true, continuous log-normal price distribution centered on the current price, the price model we developed in Equations 6-17 and 6-18 converge to the results obtained using Black/Scholes.

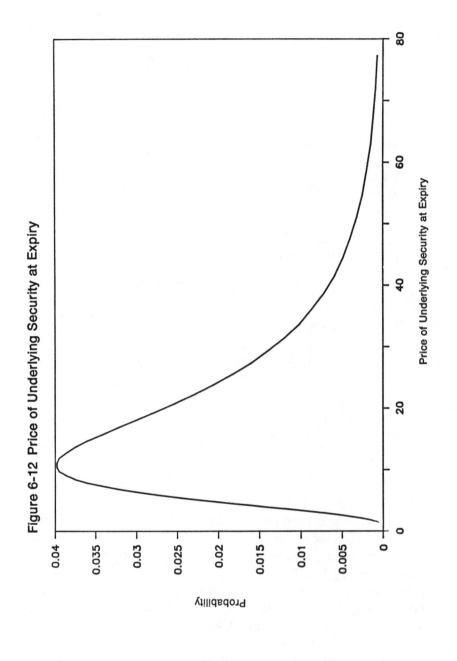

Figure 6-12 Price of Underlying Security at Expiry

Avoiding Assumptions about Risk Preference, Prediction of Rate of Return

Using a convenient, closed-form formula like the Black-Scholes has numerous advantages when its assumptions (constant r and V, no exercise before expiration, log-normal distribution of U_x) are a reasonable approximation of reality. It allows fair prices to be calculated easily. By taking the first and second derivatives of option price with respect to U_n, delta and gamma are easily. calculated as well. The formula is mechanically very convenient. However, the mechanical Black-Scholes formula as we have derived it would not have stirred much interest among academics and practitioners. This is because, as we have derived the formula, we need to know the risk-preference of option buyers and the probability of various prices prevailing at expiration. We assumed that option buyers must be risk-neutral, when it seems likely that many option users dislike uncertainty. We also assumed we know the probabilities that prices would move to various levels, when price prediction is, in fact, quite difficult.

What made the Black-Scholes model especially attractive was not the end result formula, but the way Black and Scholes derived it. They did so without making assumptions about risk preference or prediction of probable mean rate of return (and hence the mean expected price at expiration).

Black and Sholes used some rather abstruse calculus techniques to develop their model, but an alternative derivation described by Cox and Rubenstein is more easily intuited.

Consider the following situation. A security is currently priced at $10. In one period the security's price will be either $15 or $5. It is possible to borrow or lend at a rate of 10%. A call on this security has a strike price of $10 and expires in one period. The call must have a value of $2.74, regardless of the probabilities associated with the possible prices at the end of the period, and regardless of the risk preferences of option market participants. There is an arbitrage which will enforce this price:

At Expiration

	Now		$U_x = 15$		$U_x = 5$	
Action	Cashflow	Action	Cashflow	Action	Cashflow
Buy security	−10	Buy security	−15	Sell security	+5
Sell 2 calls		Calls			
@ $2.74	+5.48	exercised	20	Calls expire	0
Borrow	+4.52	Repay	−5	Repay	−5
	0		0		0

If the call price is greater than $2.74, a profit could be taken now with no risk of loss at expiration. If the call price were less than $2.74, the opposite trade (sell security, buy two calls) would result in a riskless profit. Whenever there are two possible prices at expiration, and the strike, underlying price, time to expiration, and rate of interest are known, an arbitrage is possible which will determine the price of the call:

Buy the underlying security, sell X calls and borrow B where

$$X = \frac{U_n - U_1}{C_h - C_1} \qquad (6\text{-}19a)$$

$$B = (U_h - X \times C_h) \times e^{-rt} \qquad (6\text{-}19b)$$

$$C = \frac{U_n - B}{X} \qquad (6\text{-}19c)$$

But what if the call had two periods to expiration, and the underlying security price could rise or fall by a given percent in each period? We could again figure the value of the call, but this time we would have to work backwards, calculating the value at each branch in a tree of possible prices, as depicted in Figure 6-13.

Using Equations 6-19a through 6-19c, we can determine what the call price must be at the end of period 1: If the underlying price is $13, the call must be worth $3.96; if the underlying price is $7.69, the call must be worth nothing. Given these values at the end of period 1, we can determine that the present value of the call must be $2.26 today. An arbitrage possibility ensures that this price must prevail:

Figure 6-13. Calculating the Value of Possible Prices

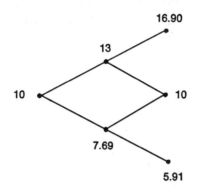

		After 1 Period			
		$U_x = 13$		$U_x = 7.69$	
Now					
Action	Cashflow	Action	Cashflow	Action	Cashflow
Buy security	−10	Sell security	+13	Sell security	7.69
Sell 1.34 calls	+3.03	Buy 1.34 calls	−5.31	Buy 1.34 calls	0
Borrow	+6.97	Repay	−7.69	Repay	−7.69
	0		0		0

As you might imagine, a binomial tree such as that in Figure 6-13 can be drawn out to many branches which may be used to reflect price changes in a day, an hour, or a minute. Each branch can represent the possibility of an up or down move of the same continuously compounded percentage. As the number of branches grows very large, the probabilities associated with various prices at expiration approaches a log-normal distribution. At this point, the unembellished binomial option price model converges to the Black-Scholes model. It does so without using any assumptions concerning risk preferences or the probabilities of up- or down- price movements.

Conclusion

This chapter is intended to give the reader an intuitive feel for option price behavior, a mechanical formula for evaluating options, and an idea of where that formula came from. The next two chapters illustrates the productive use of this information. Chapter 7 describes the major futures options contracts in use today. Chapter 8 describes a few of the many situations in which risk managers are exposed to risk because of option features embedded in securities, and how options can be used to control these and other risks.

CHAPTER 7

Analyzing Options
on Futures

Options on various futures contracts have proliferated in recent years, and in most cases have experienced spectacular growth. Their success can be attributed to several factors. First, the usefulness of the underlying futures in hedging and cross-hedging a wide variety of cash securities transfers directly to options on futures. Second, the liquidity and homogeneity of the underlying futures markets promotes efficient pricing and minimizes the risk of short-squeezes or other forms of monopolistic behavior. Finally, centralization of trading permits both futures and options thereon to be traded in close physical proximity, greatly facilitating arbitrage.

Because of the pace of innovation in the options markets, it is equally important to know how to assess the effects of option contract specifications from first principles as it is to understand the specifications of currently successful futures contracts. As with Chapter 3, this chapter will be divided into two parts. Part I offers guidelines for analysis of contract specifications. Part II applies those guidelines to specific, currently traded futures option contracts.

I. How to Assess Option Contract Specifications

Option contracts on futures generally will specify the following:

1. A system for quoting the options' premium and strike.
2. Allowed trading hours.

3. A rule to determine which strike prices are allowed.
4. Procedures governing which strike prices, on which futures delivery months, will be open for trading at any given time.
5. A rule to determine the last trading date and the expiration date of the option.
6. Rules governing exercise of the options, including:
   - When notice of exercise may be given.
   - How exercise is assigned to option writer.
   - When and how exercise results in establishment of futures positions in the accounts of the exercising option owner and the assigned option writer.

Understanding the specifications of the futures underlying given option contracts is a large part of understanding the options contracts themselves. Additional questions which must be answered include the following:

1. What system is used to describe the option—its underlying futures contract, the strike price, or the premium?
2. How is the quoted premium translated into a dollar invoice price for the option?
3. How is margin determined for short option positions?
4. How is arbitrage conducted in the options market?
5. What factors influence optimal exercise of the options?
6. Are there quirks in the exercise or expiration procedures which affect option value?
7. What conventions are used in discussing option value, delta, gamma, theta, and implied volatility?

Systems for Describing the Option

There are more variables to include in a description of an option than of a futures contract. The result is that the option symbols are more complex and less standardized than symbols for futures contracts. Most frequently a five letter code is used, for example:

CGHHF = Call on government bond futures up for delivery in March, with a strike price of 86.

> TPZJD = Put on a ten-year T-note futures up for delivery in December with a strike price of 94.

Obviously, further elucidation is required.

The most basic information to convey is the underlying futures contract. This is generally done with a single letter, the first or second in the five letter code. Sometimes the letter is logical (E for Eurodollar; T for ten-year note). Sometimes it is logical but not very descriptive (G for U.S. Government bond); and sometimes it is completely arbitrary (Q for Muni bond futures options).

The second fact to convey is whether the option being described is a put or call. P denotes put, and C, call. This letter sometimes appears first and sometimes second in the symbol. The third letter in the symbol conveys the delivery month of the underlying futures contract, and uses the same system as the futures: H for March, M for June, U for September, Z for December, etc. Notice that the delivery month does not necessarily indicate the expiration date of the option; for example, bond and note futures expire late in the month before the delivery month of the underlying futures. The last two letters of the symbol denote the option's strike price. A simple system is used on CBOT options—one letter for each digit of the percent of par strike price, with A = 1, B = 2 . . . I = 9, J = 0. Thus, CGHHF is a call on a Government T-bond futures expiring in March, with a strike price of 86 percent of par (H = 8, F = 6). On Eurodollar futures, a more obscure pricing system is often used, which will be described later in this chapter.

From Quoted to Invoice Price

CBOT options are quoted on a percent of par system, with fractions of a percent of par expressed in 64ths. Par is the face value of the cash security deliverable into the underlying futures contract, $100,000. Thus a bond or note option with a quoted premium of 1 − 32 is $100,000 × 1 32/64% = $1,500. The value of the minimum trading increment, 1/64th, is $15.625. In the Eurodollar futures options, the add-on index system is used, with each index basis point worth $25. Thus a quoted premium of .25 on a Eurodollar option translates to an invoice price of $25 × 25 or $625.

Margin on Short Futures Options

The most the buyer of an option on futures can lose is the initial premium paid for the option, since he or she can always allow the option to expire worthless. An option writer, on the other hand, is exposed to a contingent liability of indefinite size. For this reason, option writers are required to keep balances in their margin accounts which are a function of the number of options they have written and the moneyness of the options. Exchange rules specify that the minimum margin must equal the market value of the written option plus the greater of half the underlying futures margin or the underlying futures margin less half the amount by which the option is out-of-the-money.

For example, consider a bond call with a strike of 92, selling at 2-08. The underlying future is at 90-00; futures margin is $3,000 per contract.The short option margin must equal $2,125 plus the greater of

$$.5 \times \$3,000 = \$1,500$$

or

$$\$3,000 - .5 \times (92,000 - 90,000) = \$2000,$$

or $2,125 + $2,000 = $4,125. Short-option margins may be posted in Treasury bills, as in the case for futures. Variants in this rule apply to option spreads or combinations of options and futures.

Notice that the margin cash flow patterns on options are different than for the underlying futures. Consider the case of a long T-bond futures and a short call. Together, these positions are, in effect, a synthetic short put, as discussed in Chapter 6. However, the long-futures-short-call position would be margined differently than a short put, as illustrated in Table 7-1.

Options Arbitrage

Arbitrage is possible both between options with different strike prices and between options and the underlying futures contracts.

The basic option to futures arbitrage is called a *conversion* because a put and call position is established which effectively converts the options into a synthetic futures position. The conversion is a pure application of the *put/call parity* relationship described in Chapter 6.

Table 7-1 Synthetic versus Natural Short Put, 90 Strike

		Futures Margin = $3000		
Future Price	*Call Price*	*Put Price*	*Synthetic Margin*	*Put Margin*
88	250	2250	3250	5250
90	500	500	3500	3500
92	2250	250	4250	2250

In conversions, arbitragers buy calls and sell puts with the same strike price. The result is a total value function which looks like that of a long futures position. The arbitragers then neutralizes the risk of their positions by selling futures contracts. Let's take the case of a put and a call which are exactly at-the-money. If any option premium can be taken in by doing the conversion, none will have to be paid back on the option expiration date, and hence the entire premium is taken in as riskless profit. If conversions are done at a strike higher than the futures price, then the arbitragers are buying out-of-the-money calls and selling in-the-money puts, and will almost certainly receive premium on net. However, they have created synthetic long futures positions at a price which equals the strike price and have laid off their risk by selling futures at the lower current futures price. Sometime before or on expiration of the options, they will have to meet a margin calls equal to the difference between the strike and the initial futures price. To earn a profits on the trade, the arbitragers must be able to take in net premium in excess of the present value of the margin call to be made by the option expiration date.

Between options with different strike prices, a second arbitrage is possible, which is a close relative to the conversion. It is called the *box* and consists of a long call and short put at one strike price, plus a short call and long put at a different strike price. The net payor of premium in this transaction is said to buy the box, while the net recipient of premium is said to sell the box. As in a conversion, the cash flow on establishment of the box position should equal the present value of the margin flow which must occur by expiration if the option market is in no-arbitrage equilibrium.

Both the conversion and the box are fairly straightforward

applications of the put-call parity relationship discussed in Chapter 6. To work as expected, the options in either trade must not be exercised before expiration. In basic option theory, the absence of early exercise is a reasonable assumption, since an option owner exercising early captures an option's intrinsic value but destroys its time value and so is better off to sell the option rather than exercise it.

Optimal Exercise

However, the security underlying a futures option has margin flows associated with it, while the long option itself does not. If the option is deep enough in-the-money, it may be possible to exercise the option, invest the resulting margin inflow, and receive more than enough interest to offset the loss of time value in the option. The potential for profitable early exercise of an option increases its value to an option buyer. Early exercise of the short option position in a box or conversion can result in margin outflows which reduce the profit of the trade to an arbitrager.

Exercise Procedure

To exercise a futures option traded on either the CBOT or the CME, the option owner gives notice to the clearing corporation or division of the appropriate exchange by 8:00 P.M. central time. As a practical matter, exercise notice must be given through one's broker, who may require an earlier deadline for giving notice of exercise.

   The exchange then randomly selects a writer of the same option and assigns the writer for exercise. The following day, the exchange will place a long futures position into the exerciser's account at the call strike price; that evening the long position will be marked-to-market and the exerciser will receive a margin inflow. The exchange will place a short futures position into the call writer's account at the call strike price and will issue a margin call. Conversely, when a put is exercised, the exchange establishes a short position in the exerciser's account and pays margin to the exerciser. The writer of a put assigned for exercise receives a long futures position at the put strike price and must meet a margin call.

Expiration

On the expiration date, a particular contract may or may not provide for automatic exercise of in-the-money options. Eurodollar options do, while T-bond and T-note options are automatically exercised only if two or more points in-the-money at expiration.

Trading in a given option contract typically ends before the option actually expires. In consequence, close-to-the-money options typically retain some time value even at the very end of trading, since there is some possibility that the options will move further toward the money after trading terminates, but before expiration. Conversely, there are frequently willing sellers of in-the-money options at the end of trading in contracts where exercise will not be automatic, since there is a small chance that some sleepy owner of an expiring in-the-money option will not give notice of exercise before expiration.

Valuation Procedures

While pure box and conversion trades are made in the futures options markets, most market participants rely on Black-Scholes-based valuation procedures to gauge fairness of pricing and option interest sensitivity. For use on futures options, the Black-Scholes model must be modified in a couple of ways:

- The variable h should be set to zero when applying the modified Black-Scholes model presented in Chapter 6 to options on futures. This reflects the fact that futures as underlying securities neither accrue interest savings nor require financing.

- By convention, calls on futures priced on a rate index (e.g., Eurodollar futures options) are treated as puts on the rate itself rather than calls on the index price. Conversely, a put on a rate-index futures contract is treated as a call on the underlying rate. Consider a put on the June Eurodollar futures with a strike of 92-00 and an underlying price of 92-26. To evaluate this put, the formula for calls, Equation 6-2, will be used, with the following inputs:

$$S = 100 - 92.00 = 8$$
$$U = 100 - 92.26 = 7.74$$

t = Calendar days to expiration

r = A short term rate proxy

V = Implied or historical volatility of 100 — Euro Futures price (forward 90-day LIBOR)

h = 0

For options on futures which are priced on the percent-of-par method, no conversion of prices to rates and calls to puts is required.

Black-Scholes versus Reality

How well does the Black-Scholes model describe reality in the market for futures options? As a theoretical model, Black-Scholes does not hold up very well.

The one testable implication of the model is that market expectations concerning the volatility of underlying securities will remain constant over time. As you will recall, the positive or negative return must be the same at each branch of the binomial price tree of the underlying security in order for the distribution of price at expiration to approach a log-normal shape. This, in turn, implies that the volatility of the underlying security must be constant over time.

An examination of implied volatilities in efficient markets should reveal that all puts and calls on a given underlying security have the same implied volatility regardless of strike, time to expiration, or the time at which they are observed.

Yet this is far from the case. Options with the same expiration date but different strikes typically have higher implied volatilities the farther in- or out-of-the-money they are. The market seems to assign higher probability to large changes in underlying price than allowed for under the log-normal distribution assumption. Puts of all strikes will often have persistently higher or lower implied volatilities than calls on a given underlying security. Often, options on a given underlying security with a long time to expiration will have different implied volatilities than options with shorter times to expiration. In all options, implied volatilities vary dramatically over time, as illustrated in Figure 7-1.

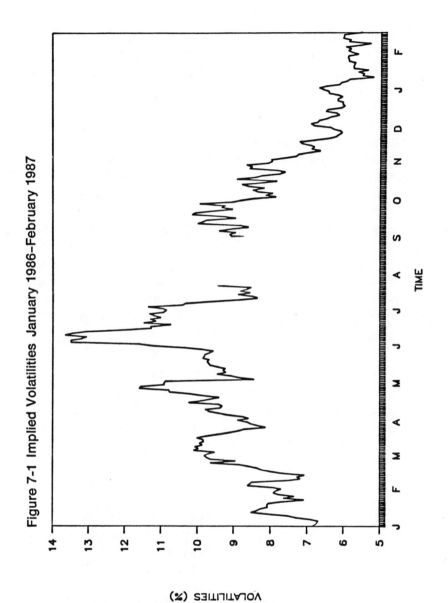

Figure 7-1 Implied Volatilities January 1986–February 1987

One might argue that these perceived problems reflect market inefficiencies, rather than the inadequacy of Black-Scholes to describe option behavior in an efficient market. If that were the case, a trader who understood Black-Scholes would be able to devise strategies to identify and exploit pricing inefficiency, based on the use of implied volatility. Yet, consistently profitable strategies based on implied volatility remain elusive.

Ultimately, the usefulness of the Black-Scholes model depends not so much on its attractiveness as a theoretical model but on how closely it predicts actual option prices and price sensitivity in practice. In practice, the Black-Scholes formula can be used to predict quite accurately the price and price sensitivity of puts and calls which are not too far away from the money or too near or far from expiration. Viewed as a useful rule of thumb rather than as an object of worship, the Black-Scholes formula can be invaluable in the valuation of exchange traded options and in designing option strategies for rate risk management.

II. Currently Traded Options on Futures

Contract: **Options on Eurodollar Futures**

Symbol:

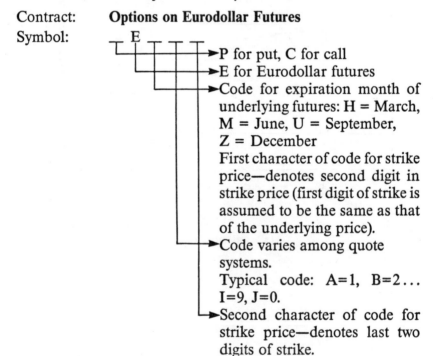

E

➤ P for put, C for call

➤ E for Eurodollar futures

➤ Code for expiration month of underlying futures: H = March, M = June, U = September, Z = December

First character of code for strike price—denotes second digit in strike price (first digit of strike is assumed to be the same as that of the underlying price).

➤ Code varies among quote systems. Typical code: A=1, B=2... I=9, J=0.

➤ Second character of code for strike price—denotes last two digits of strike.

Typical code: A=05, B=10,...
E=25 ... J=50 ... O=75 ...
T=00.

Examples:
PEUBJ: Sep. 92.50 Euro Put
CEHCO: March 93.75 Euro Call

Strike Prices: Every 25 add-on index basis points for strikes above 91.00; every 50 basis points for strikes below 91.00. Examples of allowable strikes include 90.00, 90.50, 91.00, 91.25, 91.50, 91.75, etc.

Trading Hours: 7:20 A.M. to 2:00 P.M. central time.

Expiration: On the same day the underlying futures contract expires; typically, the Monday preceding the third Wednesday of the futures expiration month. Trading ceases at 10:00 A.M. central time on the expiration day; expiration itself occurs at 5:00 P.M. Trading is allowed in options up to nine months from expiration.

Exercise: Notice given to the clearing division of the CME by 8:00 P.M. central time results in a futures position (long for calls, short for puts) in the exerciser's account at the exercised option's strike price on the following trading day. Because the underlying futures expires on the same day, exercise at expiration results in no futures position, but only a margin flow on the following trading day. Exercise is automatic for all in-the-money options at expiration.

Valuation Procedure: The add-on index equals 100 minus the add-on rate of the deliverable Eurodollar time deposit. By convention, calls on Eurodollar futures are analyzed as puts on Eurodollar rates (90-day LIBOR), and puts on Euro futures are treated as calls on 90-day LIBOR. To use the modified Black-Scholes formula to evaluate Eurodollar options:

1. Set t (time to expiration) equal to fraction of a year (actual/actual basis) from the trade date to the expiration date.
2. Set r (the short-term rate) to the current 90-day T-bill rate or other short term rate proxy (Black-Scholes is fairly insensitive to rate assumptions if time to expiration is relatively short).
3. Set S (the strike) equal to 100 minus the quoted strike.
4. Set U (the underlying price) equal to 100 minus the quoted underlying futures price.
5. Set V (volatility) to the annualized historical or implied rate volatility for 90 day LIBOR.
6. If the option to be evaluated is a call on a Euro futures, use the Black-Scholes formula for puts; if the option is a put on a Euro futures, use the Black-Scholes formula for calls. For all futures options, set h to zero in the Black-Scholes formula.

By convention, services which supply implied volatility on Eurodollar options quote the volatility of the rate, not of the add-on index. Most use a 260-day convention for annualization of volatility but actual days for time to expiration.

Contract: **Ten-Year Note Futures Option**

Symbol:

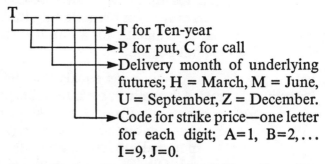

T for Ten-year
P for put, C for call
Delivery month of underlying futures; H = March, M = June, U = September, Z = December.
Code for strike price—one letter for each digit; A=1, B=2,... I=9, J=0.

Strike Prices: Every whole percent of par. Allowable strike prices include ... 80, 81, 82 ..., etc. The CBOT opens trading on options three strikes in- and out-of-the-money at any time.

Trading Hours: Trading starts at 5:00 P.M. central time the evening before a given trade date and is suspended at 8:30 P.M.; trading then resumes from 8:00 A.M. to 2:00 P.M. central time on the trading day itself. When Daylight Savings Time is in effect, the evening session hours are from 6:00 to 9:30 P.M.

Expiration: The last day of trading is the last Friday at least five business days before the first day on which notice of delivery may be given on the underlying T-note futures contract (first notice day is the second business day before the start of the delivery month). Trading ceases at noon on the last trading day. The contract does not expire until 10:00 A.M. the day after trading stops. Trading is allowed on options up to nine months from expiration.

Exercise: Notice of exercise may be given until 8:00 P.M. Central time on any trading day. The clearing corporation of the CBOT then randomly assigns exercise to a writer of the option. The following trading day, the exercising call owner has a long futures position placed in his account and receives a margin inflow when the contract is marked-to-market; the assigned call writer has a short futures position placed in his account and meets a margin call when the short position is marked-to-market. Conversely, the exerciser of a put has a short futures position placed in his account at the strike price, while the assigned put writer gets a long futures position at the strike price.

Valuation Procedure: No quirks of convention complicate the evaluation of options on T-note futures. As inputs to the Black-Scholes model, set

S = quoted strike price

U = quoted underlying futures price

t = fraction of a year to expiration (actual/actual basis)

r = short term rate proxy (T-bill rate)

h = 0 (zero)

V = annualized historical or implied volatility

Use the Black-Scholes call price formula for calls and the put price formula for puts.

Contract:	**Treasury Bond Futures Option**
Symbol:	

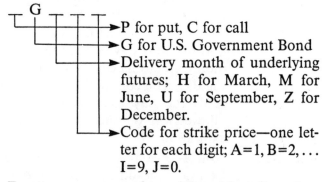

→ P for put, C for call

→ G for U.S. Government Bond

→ Delivery month of underlying futures; H for March, M for June, U for September, Z for December.

→ Code for strike price—one letter for each digit; A=1, B=2, ... I=9, J=0.

Strike Prices:	Every even percent of par. Allowable strike prices include 80, 82, 84, 86, 88, 90. The CBOT opens trading on options three strikes in- and out-of-the money at any time.
Trading Hours:	Trading starts at 5:00 P.M. central time the evening before a given trade date and is suspended at 8:30 P.M.; trading then resumes from 8:00 A.M. to 2:00 P.M. central time on the trading day itself. When Daylight Savings Time is in effect, evening session hours are from 6:00 to 9:30 P.M.
Expiration:	The last day of trading is the last Friday at least five business days before the first day on which notice of delivery may be given on the underlying T-note futures contract (first notice day is the second business day before the start of the delivery month). Trading ceases at noon on the last trading day. The contract does not expire until 10:00 A.M. the day after trading stops. Trading is allowed on options up to nine months from expiration.

Exercise: Notice of exercise may be given until 8:00 P.M. Central time on a trading day. The clearing corporation of the CBOT then randomly assigns exercise to a writer of the option. The following trading day, the exercising call owner has a long futures position placed in his or her account and receives a margin inflow when the contract is marked-to-market; the assigned call writer has a short futures position placed in his or her account and meets a margin call when the short position is marked-to-market. Conversely, the exerciser of a put has a short futures position placed in his or her account at the strike price, while the assigned put writer gets a long futures position at the strike price.

Valuation No quirks of convention complicate the evaluation of options on T-bond futures. As inputs to the Black-Scholes model, set
Procedure:

S = quoted strike price

U = quoted underlying futures price

t = fraction of a year to expiration (actual/actual basis)

r = short term rate proxy (T-bill rate)

h = 0 (zero)

V = annualized historical or implied volatility

Use the Black-Scholes call price formula for calls and the put price formula for puts.

Contract: **Municipal Bond Index Futures Option**

Symbol:

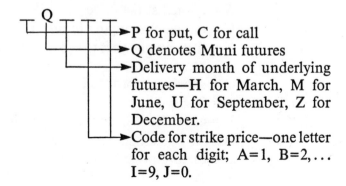

Q

→P for put, C for call

→Q denotes Muni futures

→Delivery month of underlying futures—H for March, M for June, U for September, Z for December.

→Code for strike price—one letter for each digit; A=1, B=2, . . . I=9, J=0.

Strike Prices: Every even percent of par. Allowable strike prices include 80, 82, 84, 86, 88, 90. The CBOT opens trading on options three strikes in- and out-of-the-money at any time.

Trading Hours: 8:00 A.M. to 2:00 P.M. central time.

Expiration: Currently, expiration and the last day of trading occur on the eighth last business day of the delivery month. The contract stops trading at 2:00 P.M. and expires at 8:00 P.M. central time. Trading is allowed on options up to nine months from expiration.

Exercise: Notice of exercise may be given until 8:00 P.M. central time on a trading day. The clearing corporation of the CBOT then randomly assigns exercise to a writer of the option. The following trading day, the exercising call owner has a long futures position placed in his account and receives a margin inflow when the contract is marked-to-market; the assigned call writer has a short futures position placed in his account and meets a margin call when the short position is marked-to-market. Conversely, the exerciser of a put has a short futures position placed in his account at the strike price, while the assigned put writer gets a long futures position at the strike price.

Valuation Procedure. No quirks of convention complicate the evaluation of options on Muni futures. As inputs to the Black-Scholes model, set

S = quoted strike price

U = quoted underlying futures price

T = fraction of a year to expiration (actual/actual basis)

r = short term proxy (T-bill rate)

h = 0 (zero)

V = annualized historical or implied volatility

Use the Black-Scholes call price formula for calls and the put price formula for puts.

CHAPTER 8

Uses of Options and Option Theory in Risk Management

Gamma is the miracle drug of rate risk management, continually increasing an option's capacity to profit in favorable markets while reducing its susceptibility to loss under adverse conditions. Risk managers buy options for their gamma to limit risk but not profit potential or to offset the negative gamma of other securities. Risk managers with gamma to spare sell options when they fetch an attractive price in the market.

This chapter illustrates the use of options in a number of situations: simple *delta-neutral* hedging, hedging securities with embedded option features, and in the creation of various rate sensitivity profiles via combinations of options and futures. The chapter will also demonstrate the importance of the option concepts introduced in Chapter 6 in devising sensible, effective option-based hedge strategies.

Delta-Neutral Hedging

A simple basis point value matched hedge can be constructed using put options as well as futures and offers the additional advantage of creating a positive gamma for the hedged position. This type of hedge is often referred to as a *delta-neutral* hedge in puts. To delta-neutral hedge a security using futures options, calculate the BPV of the cash security and of the futures underlying the option contract. Determine the number of futures contracts required to hedge the cash security in futures. Next, calculate the delta of the put to be used, and divide the quantity of futures required in a futures hedge by the negative of the delta of the put. The result is the quantity of options to buy:

$$\# \text{ Puts} = \frac{\text{BPV cash}}{\text{BPV futures}} \, / \, (-\text{delta}_p) \qquad (8\text{-}1a)$$

As an example, consider hedging \$1 million of the 8⅞ Treasury bond maturity August 15, 2017 on January 13, 1988, using March 86 T-bond puts.

Cash Price: 97.18   BPV: 997.70
USH Price: 87-00   BPV:89.59 (factored)
(Cheapest to deliver: 7⅛ of 5/15/2016, CF = .9167)
March 86 Bond Put Price: 1-22   Delta: −.40   Gamma: .09

$$\# \text{ Puts} = \frac{997.70}{89.59} \, / \, .40 = 27.8 \text{ March 86 Puts}$$

Notice some important features of this delta-neutral hedge. First, the hedge is neutral only for relatively small moves around the current price. A large down move in bond prices would move the puts into-the-money, raising their delta and causing the put position to gain in value more than the loss on the cash bond. Conversely, a large rise in bond prices will move the puts out-of-the-money, reducing their deltas and causing the put position to lose less than the gain on the cash bonds. The total value of the hedge position is depicted in Figure 8-1a.

> **Large changes in price, up or down,**
> *profit a delta-neutral hedge in puts.*

This pleasant scenario ignores the cost of delta-neutral hedging, the tendency of the market value of the puts to decline as they approach expiration. This time decay will cause the total value line in Figure 8-1a to decline slowly over time, leaving the position with a net decline in value equal to the total put premium paid, if market prices have not changed by expiration.

Much effort is expended by hedgers to determine whether it is more desirable to buy at-the-money and/or soon-to-expire puts which have relatively high gamma but also a higher rate of time decay, or to buy away-from-the-money, far-from-expiration options with a relatively low rate of time decay. The conventional wisdom dictates that at some point it is wise to sell off front-

Figure 8-1a Delta-Neutral Put Hedge

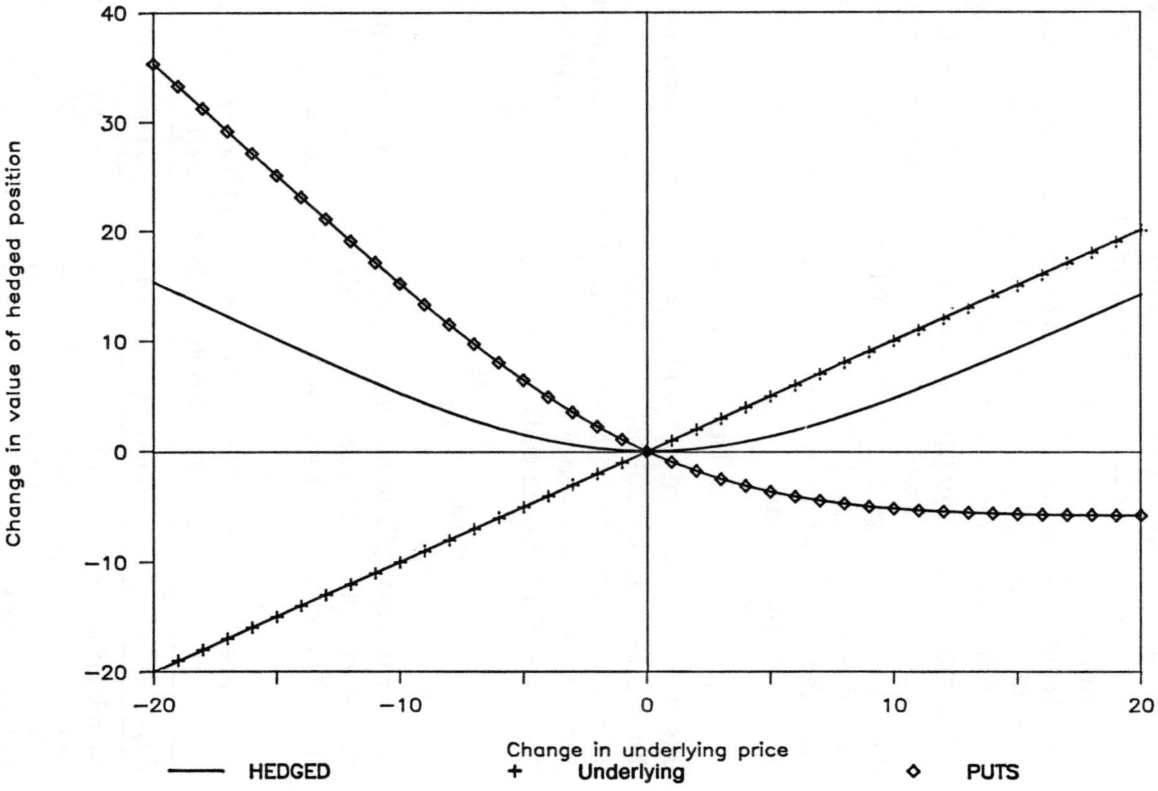

Change in value of hedged position

Change in underlying price

— HEDGED   + Underlying   ◇ PUTS

month puts and replace them with deferred-month puts to avoid the increasing rate of time decay in the front-month options.

However, there is a direct association between time decay and gamma; in fact, time decay can be thought of as *gamma rent*. Viewed in this way, there is often little advantage to choosing options with longer times to expiration as opposed to shorter; what differences there are in gamma rent often seem to correlate well with differences in the amount of premium required to purchase the option, as suggested in Table 8-1. In a world with commissions and bid-asked spreads, perhaps the best strategy is to find the option which will give the desired gamma with the lowest transaction cost.

Delta-Neutral Call Writing

Just as a BPV-matched hedge of an asset can be constructed by buying puts, a hedge can be constructed by selling calls. To determine the number of calls to sell, calculate the number of futures required in a futures hedge, then divide the number of futures by the delta of the chosen calls.

$$\# \text{ calls} = \frac{\text{BPV cash}}{\text{BPV shares}} \ / \ \text{delta}_c \qquad (8\text{-}1b)$$

By writing calls to hedge, the hedger takes in the premium on the sold calls. If market prices decline modestly, the value of the calls declines, producing a profit on the short-call position,

Table 8-1 Gamma Rent of Various Puts, 13 January 1988
(Futures: USH = 87-00   USM = 86-01)

Expiry	Strike	Price	Gamma Rent*
March (38 days)	80	0-07	$4.46
March	86	0-34	$2.73
March	92	3-16	$2.68
June (129 days)	80	0-50	$3.72
June	86	1-63	$2.23
June	92	5-11	$2.23

*Equals expected dollar decay in premium per day divided by the option's gamma times 100
Source: Bloomberg L.P.

which offsets the loss on the hedged cash asset. If market prices decline substantially, the short calls move away from the money, and their delta moves toward zero. As a result, the call position profits do not offset the cash loss, and the total hedge position loses value.

Conversely, in a substantial rise in market prices, the calls move into the money and their deltas rise; the short calls generate a loss which exceeds the gain on the hedged cash asset. The total payoff function is depicted in Figure 8-1b. As consolation for the grim payoff function, a delta-neutral call writing strategy permits the hedger to capture and keep time premium in quiet markets as the calls' time premium decays until expiration.

Portfolio Insurance

The concept behind portfolio insurance is simply that the exposure of an option for small moves in price can be matched by buying or selling delta futures per option. The hedger who otherwise might wish to buy a futures put could instead sell ($-\text{delta}_p$) futures, and adjust continually as the delta of the put changed. Provided that the futures market stays liquid, the hedger could in principle replicate the effects of owning a put, but avoid paying time premium. On the other hand, each change in market levels necessitates a transaction with its attendant costs; further, the most transactions will be required when the market is moving at its fastest, when conditions are likely to be illiquid.

Pros and Cons

Is there an obviously superior choice between buying puts, selling calls, or portfolio insurance for the asset hedger? While the put buyer must pay an often sizable premium initially to create a delta-neutral hedge in puts, periodic large changes in prices produce gains in the hedged position, which can be locked in when the hedger adjusts the put position to restore delta-neutrality. Over time, these gains tend to offset time decay in the put premium, so that in the end, relatively little is paid for option protection. Conversely, while substantial premium is taken in initially by call writers, periodic large moves in rates result in losses to the hedged position which, over time, appear to offset the premium taken in.

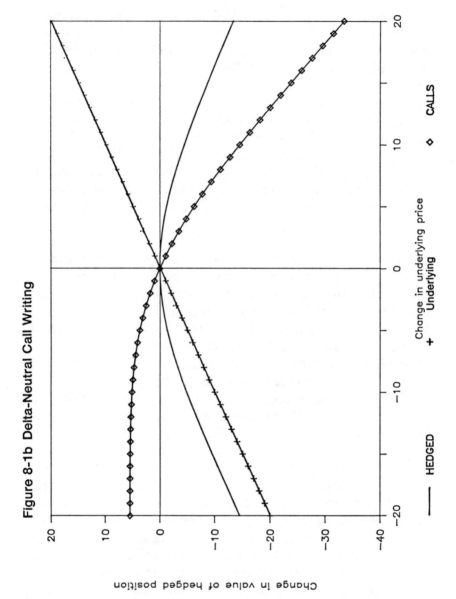

Figure 8-1b Delta-Neutral Call Writing

Change in value of hedged position

Change in underlying price

+ Underlying   ◇ CALLS   —— HEDGED

Portfolio insurance rests critically on the assumptions of continuous, small price changes, liquid markets, and low transaction costs. In practice, it is difficult to adjust a futures position precisely in reaction to small price changes, and a net loss relative to a comparable put hedge is incurred in a portfolio insurance strategy when prices move a larger amount between position adjustments. This cost can be gauged based on expected market volatility; however, unpleasant surprises can occur if actual volatility exceeds expectations.

As portfolio insurers of equities discovered on October 19, 1987, futures trading can become illiquid in fast markets, just as rapid adjustments become critically important. The dramatic failure of portfolio insurance to provide price protection, and its role in greasing the skids in the October 19 stock market crash, has largely discredited the strategy.

Hedging Securities with Embedded Options: Mortgages

Many of the most common fixed income securities bought or sold in the market are actually bundles of fixed-income securities and long- or short-option positions. Understanding the behavior of each component of such a security is prerequisite to understanding the price behavior of the entire security.

Options and option features are ubiquitous in the mortgage banking business. They are encountered in the origination process and are an integral part of mortgages and mortgage-backed securities. An examination of rate risk in mortgages thus serves to illustrate the effects of option features on security price behavior.

The Prepayment Feature

Most mortgages carry a provisions that the borrowers can prepay the remaining principal balance on the mortgage at any time without penalty. These rights to prepay are call options owned by the borrower; if it is to his advantage, he can call an IOU—the mortgage—from the lender at an exercise price equal to the unamortized principal balance on the loan. If new mortgage rates fall below the rate on an existing mortgage, the prepayment option moves into the money. This option has time value as well as intrinsic value, so the mortgagee may not prepay if his mortgage rate is only a little higher than market rates.

However, if market rates fall far enough, the mortgagee will pay off his existing mortgage and obtain a new mortgage at a lower rate. Conversely, if a mortgage carries a below-market rate, the mortgagee will not choose to prepay and refinance at higher market rates. The mortgage lender, therefore, is the owner of a covered write position. He is long an asset, which pays a stream of, for example, 360 monthly payments, but is short a call on that asset. As is the case for a covered write, the value of the lender's position will change similarly to the value of a 30-year-fixed-income security, if market rates are well above the rate on the mortgage; but the value will become less and less rate sensitive if market rates fall, and the prepayment call moves into-the-money. For writing a prepayment option, the mortgage lender is compensated through points paid by the borrower at the time the mortgage is closed.

The owner of a mortgage-backed security is in much the same position as the lender originating a single mortgage. If the rates on the pool of mortgages backing the security substantially exceed current market rates, a large fraction of the mortgages will be prepaid, and these prepayments will be passed through to the security owner, substantially diminishing the return realized on the security.

Assuming that the delta of the prepayment option on a mortgage or mortgage-backed security could be calculated accurately, the basis point value of the mortgage or security would be easy to determine:

$$BPV_m = BPV_a - BPV_c \qquad (8\text{-}2)$$

where

BPV_m = Basis point value of total mortgage or mortgage backed security

BPV_c = Basis point value of the prepayment call option

BPV_a = Basis point value of the stream of amortizations associated with the mortgage, assuming no prepayment.

One might try to use the Black-Scholes formulas discussed earlier to evaluate the prepayment option. However, the option is more complex than the type assumed by the formulas. The strike price declines each month as principal amortization occurs, and mortgagees may not prepay optimally, prepaying when market rates are high because of death, divorce, or job transfer, or failing to prepay when rates are low because of ignorance or inability to obtain refinancing.

In practice, an empirical approach to estimating mortgage interest sensitivity may prove the most reliable. Whatever empirically estimated model is used should be consistent with option concepts. If a mortgage or mortgage-backed security is selling near par, the estimated interest sensitivity should be approximately half the sensitivity of the associated amortization stream, assuming no prepayment. If the security is selling well below par, its interest sensitivity should approach that of the amortization stream, assuming no (rate-related) prepayment; if the security is selling at a substantial premium, its interest sensitivity should be very low.

The traditional approach to evaluating mortgage security value and interest sensitivity is to make an assumption about when the backing mortgages will prepay, and then to evaluate the cash flows which would result using the Treasury yield curve. Prepayment assumptions range from very simple (all mortgages will prepay on a given future date) to rather elaborate (certain benchmark pools experienced a particular pattern of prepayment, and the mortgage pool being evaluated is assumed to prepay at some percentage of the experience of the benchmark pool).

If the cash flows including prepayments on a given pool were very carefully predicted, and the present value of the cash flows calculated, using a given interest rate scenario, the resulting estimated pool value would exceed the going market price of the security backed by the pool. Such a calculation takes into account the intrinsic value, but not the time value, of the prepayment option. Because the prepayment option in fact does have time value, the market value of the mortgage will be less than the present value of the projected cash flows. By the same token, interest sensitivity calculations based on projected cash flows will tend to overstate mortgage security interest sensitivity, since they will ignore the behavior of the time value component of prepayment option value.

In hedging the value of mortgage pools and mortgage-backed securities, the prepayment option will make the pool or security BPV much more sensitive to changes in rates than securities without option features. A cross-hedge in Treasury note or bond futures therefore must be adjusted more frequently for the effects of rate changes. The hedge will be most sensitive when the mortgages are near par, since the prepayment option there is close to the money, and the option delta changes most rapidly in response to rate changes. The hedge ratio will be more stable for mortgage securities selling at a large discount or premium.

A simulation of the results of such a hedge of FHLMC PCs during 1986 yields acceptable if unspectacular results on both low and high coupon PCs, as shown in Figures 8-2 and 8-3. These hedges were attained not by using a static futures position, but one which was adjusted depending on the price of the PC and of the note futures. As PC prices rose, less futures were required to hedge. Less futures were needed to hedge the high-coupon PC than the lower-coupon PC, as indicated in Figures 8-4 and 8-5.

There is an inherent flaw to the approach of using only futures to hedge a mortgage-backed security. As interest rates enter turbulent periods, option premiums tend to rise. Thus, the embedded short call in a mortgage security rises in price, depressing mortgage prices relative to Treasury prices. Treasury futures can control the effects of changing rates, but not changing volatility.

Using puts to hedge mortgage-backed securities confers two advantages compared to futures: the puts become more sensitive to rate changes as rates rise, just as mortgage securities do; and puts increase in value when the market perception of volatility increases, countering the tendency of mortgage securities to fall in value relative to Treasuries when volatility increases.

Consider the example presented in Figures 8-6 through 8-8. Figure 8-6 depicts a hedge of GNMA 8% PCs during 1986. The hedged position expressed a large basis loss in May and June and a subsequent long, slow basis gain. Figure 8-7 shows implied volatility of T-rate options over the same period; note that a large jump in volatility coincides perfectly with the May-June hedge

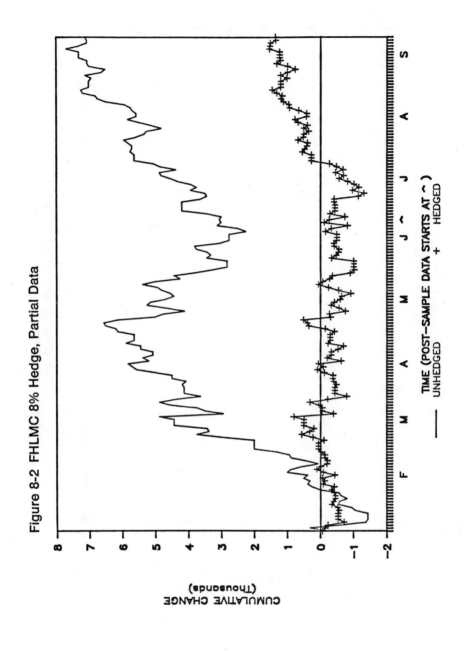

Figure 8-2 FHLMC 8% Hedge, Partial Data

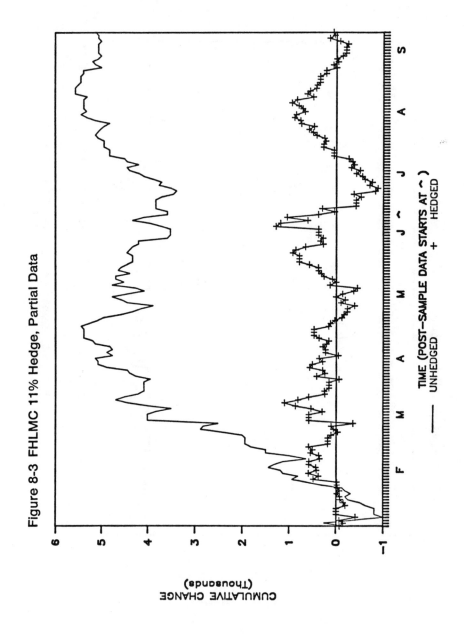

Figure 8-3 FHLMC 11% Hedge, Partial Data

CUMULATIVE CHANGE
(Thousands)

TIME (POST–SAMPLE DATA STARTS AT ⌃)
——— UNHEDGED   + HEDGED

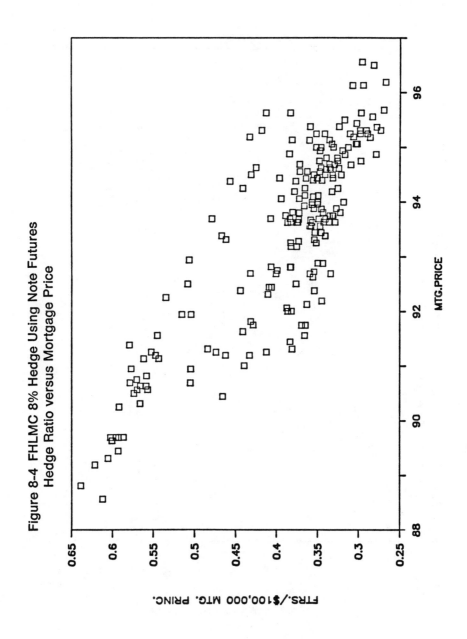

Figure 8-4 FHLMC 8% Hedge Using Note Futures
Hedge Ratio versus Mortgage Price

Figure 8-5 FHLMC 11% Hedge Using Note Futures
Hedge Ratio versus Mortgage Price

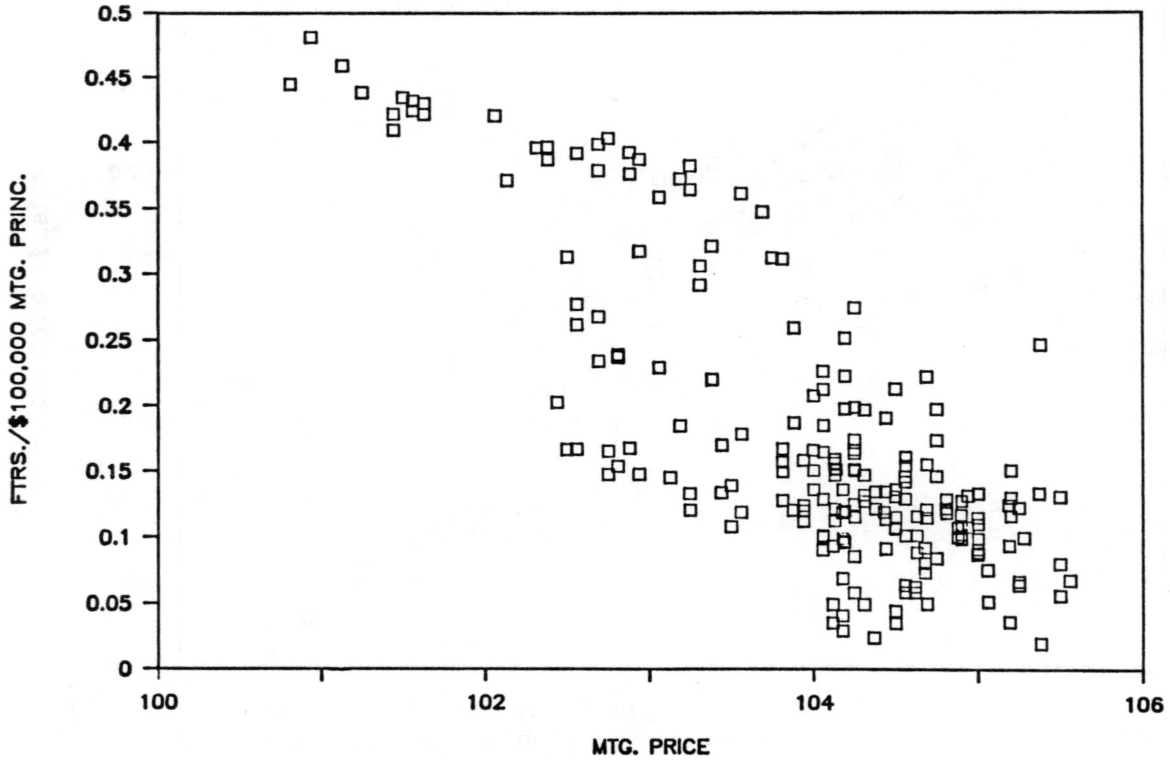

Figure 8-6 GNMA 8% Hedge in Note Futures
January 1986–February 1987

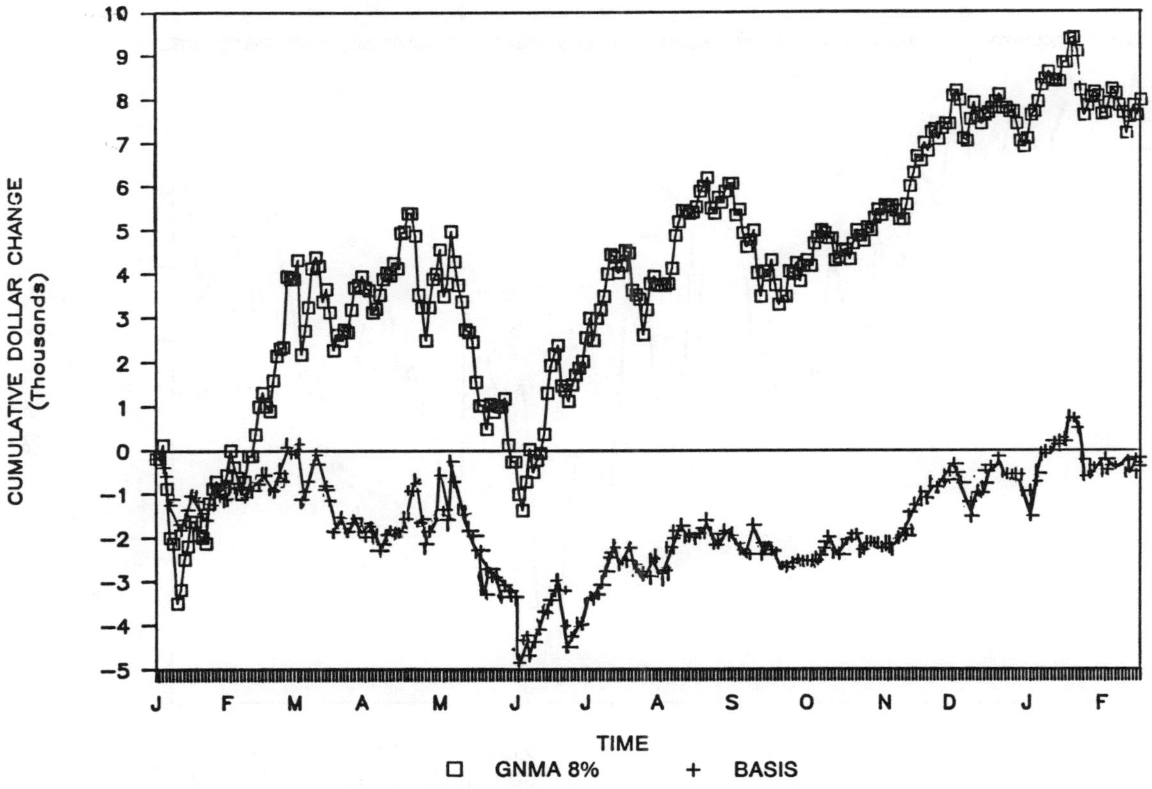

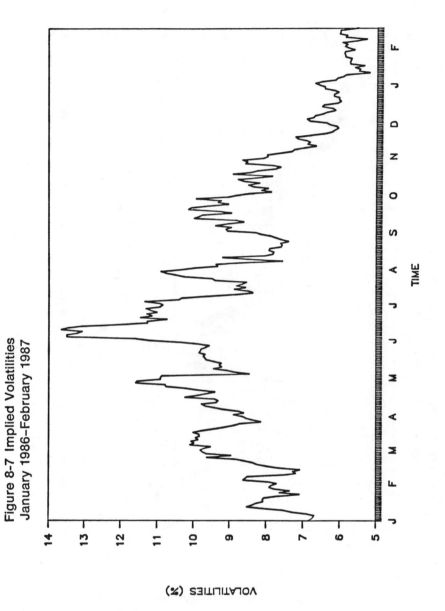

Figure 8-7 Implied Volatilities
January 1986–February 1987

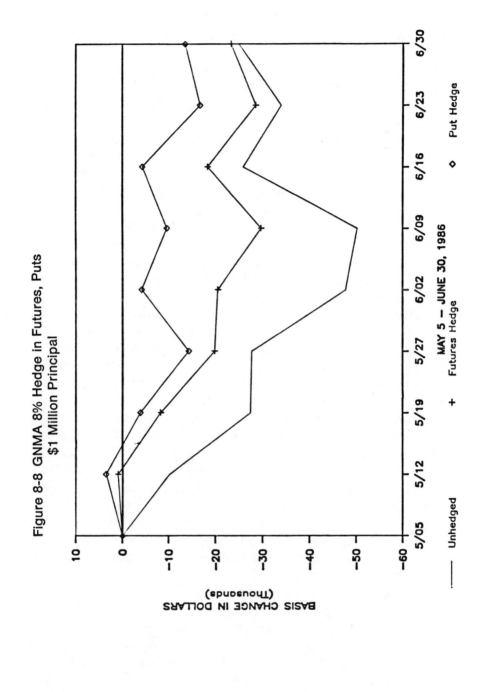

Figure 8-8 GNMA 8% Hedge in Futures, Puts
$1 Million Principal

loss, while the subsequent gradual decline in volatility coincides with a gradual gain on the hedge position. Figure 8-8 compares the performance of a hedge in futures to a hedge in puts over the troubling May-June period. The puts, benefiting from increased volatility, do a better job offsetting the decline in the PCs price than do the futures.

An important innovation in the mortgage banking industry is the introduction of the adjustable rate mortgage (ARM). In a typical ARM, an initial rate is set and an amortization schedule is calculated as for a normal fixed rate mortgage, for example, assuming 30 years of monthly amortizations at the initial rate. A provision is made in the mortgage for adjustment of the rate at regular intervals; for example, once per year. Eleven months after the mortgage is closed, a benchmark rate, such as the one year T-bill rate, is observed and a new mortgage rate is set. The following month, a new amortization schedule is established, based on the unamortized principal balance at that time, the new rate, and 29 years of monthly amortization. The adjustment process is repeated annually over the life of the ARM. To protect the borrower from unaffordable increases in his mortgage rate, ARMs usually incorporate limits on the amount by which the mortgage rate can change. A typical provision would be that the rate can change a maximum of 2% at each adjustment and can rise a maximum of 5% from the initial rate any time during the life of the mortgage.

Institutions attempting to hedge a portfolio of ARMs have been frequently dismayed by their experience. They found that while note or bill futures rallied by large amounts, the ARMs being hedged increased in value very little, resulting in large net losses on the hedges. The poor hedge performances resulted from a failure to understand the option features implicit in typical ARMs.

At its core, an ARM is an adjustable rate security. Thus, while its legal life might be 30 years, its duration is a function of the time until the next rate adjustment. At that point, we assume that the mortgage is paid off and replaced immediately by a new mortgage. One component of ARM interest sensitivity, then, is the BPV of amortizations to the next adjustment, plus the BPV of a prepayment of unamortized principal on the adjustment date.

A second component of ARM interest sensitivity is introduced by limitations placed on the amount by which the mortgage rate can be adjusted. A 2% limit on each rate adjustment represents a put option held by the borrower; if market rates rise above the maximum upward adjustment allowed on the ARM, the borrower in effect is able to put his IOU to the lender at a rate below market rates for the next adjustment interval. The security underlying this put is the stream of amortizations payable between the next adjustment and the adjustment after the next one, plus the unamortized principal at the end of this period, at the maximum allowed rate. The put option is in-the-money if the forward rate from the next adjustment to the one following is higher than the maximum rate allowed under the terms of the ARM.

This put feature causes ARM interest sensitivity to shrink in a falling rate environment and to increase in a rising rate environment. From the lender's viewpoint, if rates are low and likely to change by a small amount, he will probably be able to adjust the ARM rate to reflect fully any change in the benchmark rate. A one-year ARM in this environment behaves like a one-year security. If rates appear likely to rise by a large enough amount, the lender is committed to lend for the second year at a below-market rate. It now appears that the ARM carries a fixed rate for not one, but two years. As a result, the BPV of the ARM rises as rates rise.

Table 8-2 shows the modeled price behavior of a one-year ARM with an initial rate of nine percent and a two percent maximum rate change per adjustment. The period for which the ARM is modeled is one in which the yield curve dropped and flattened, i.e. in which the put feature moved out-of-the-money. This table also shows the positions and results of a hedge in bill and note futures, matched for BPV and SPV. Notice that the interest sensitivity of the ARM declined over the period, requiring several adjustments to the futures position to maintain an accurate hedge. As with any security having an embedded option feature, a large rapid market move detunes a hedge of the security, creating a basis loss before the hedge can be adjusted.

Table 8-2 ARM Hedge Simulation

Mortgage Characteristics

Commitment Date: 2/28/85
Estimated Closing Date: 3/30/85
Estimated Sale Date: 8/30/85
Principal: $10,000,000
Next rate adjustment date: 2/28/86
Next adjustment effective: 3/30/86
Final Maturity Date: 3/30/15
Months between adjustments: 12
Initial Rate: 9%
Index: 1-year Treasury
Markup over index: 2%
Max. Rate change per adjustment: 2%

Date	Percent Par Sale Dale Val.	BPV	SPV	TBU85 Qty	TBU85 Price	TYU85 Qty	TYU85 Price
3/30/85	98.75	761	11324	−31	90.88	−2	78-20
4/30/85	99.18	657	7996	−27	91.48	−1	80-01
5/30/85	100.03	514	1052	−22	92.55	−1	—
6/30/85	100.11	509	855	−22	—	0	85-28
7/30/85	100.19	490	883	−22	—	0	—
8/30/85	100.20	505	586	0	92.96	0	—

$$\frac{\text{Gain on ARM}}{\text{Loss on Futures}} = \frac{144,623}{149,925} = 104\%$$

Portfolios of Options

A portfolio of options can be designed to create a particular rate sensitivity profile. Suppose that a hedger wishes to own a call on a $1 million face value security which has a basis point value of $1,000. The delta of the desired call is .50 and the gamma is .03 per 1 percent change in the security's price. For a small change in rates, the basis point value of the call is

$$\text{BPV} = \$1000 \times .5 = \$500.$$

A basis point change in rates changes the underlying security price by $1000, or $1000/1,000,000 = 0.1 percent of par. The change in the delta from a one basis point change in rates will equal the gamma times the underlying price change in percent of par, $0.1 \times .03 = .003$.

The change in basis point value of the call due to a one basis point change in rates (ΔBPV) will, therefore, equal

$$\Delta BPV = \$1000 \times .003 = \$3.$$

An option with these characteristics is not available; however, you can replicate the BPV and ΔBPV of the desired call using two exchange traded calls:

Underlying Security: USH Price: 87.00   Factored BPV: 89.60

Strike	Delta	Percent of par Gamma	BPV	Underlying BPV, in Percent of Par	ΔBPV
86	.59	.09	52.86	.0896	$89.60 \times .0896 \times .09 = .72$
88	.41	.09	36.74	.0896	$89.60 \times .0896 \times .09 = .72$

To mimic the BPV and ΔBPV of the desired call, the hedger must satisfy two constraints. The basis point value of the calls bought or sold must sum to $500, the BPV of the desired call. The ΔBPVs of the calls bought or sold must sum to $3, the ΔBPV of the desired call.

$$Q_{86} \times 52.86 + Q_{88} \times 36.74 = 500$$

$$Q_{86} \times .72 + Q_{88} \times .72 = 3$$

To satisfy these constraints, the hedger must buy $Q_{86} = 21.5$ of the 86 calls and you must sell $Q_{88} = (-)17.4$ of the 88 calls. Notice that the resulting portfolio does not behave like a single call over a wide range of prices. The value of the portfolio as a function of the underlying futures price is graphed in Figure 8-9.

A portfolio which behaves more like the desired call over a wider range of prices could be constructed using one of the calls and the underlying futures, assuming that the delta of the futures is 1.0 and its gamma is zero:

$$Q_F \times 89.60 + Q_{88} \times 36.74 = 500$$

$$Q_F \times 0 + Q_{88} \times .72 = 3.$$

The hedger would buy $Q_F = 3.9$ futures and $Q_{88} = 4.2$ of the

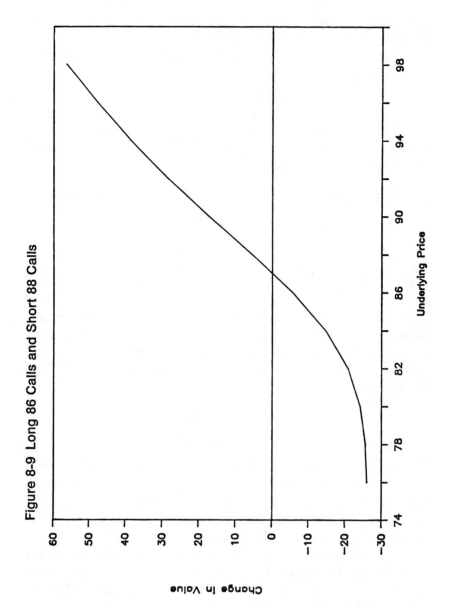

Figure 8-9 Long 86 Calls and Short 88 Calls

calls to mimic the desired call using these two securities. The result would behave more like a single call over a wider range of prices, as shown in Figure 8-10. Note that whichever strategy is chosen, the time decay characteristics of the chosen strategy have not been considered and, in all likelihood, will be different from those of the desired call. This in turn implies that the chosen strategy will have to be rebalanced periodically to control for the effects of passing time on delta and gamma.

Commitments, Caps, and Collars

Financial intermediaries now offer a variety of financial products which are in essence options or option portfolios. Among them are commitments to make fixed-rate loans at a guaranteed maximum rate, caps on the maximum rate changed on floating-rate loans, and collars in which the borrower on a floating-rate loan receives a cap in exchange for accepting a floor on his borrowing costs. Buyers of these products need to know how to evaluate them, and lenders must know how to price them and lay off the risk they represent.

A commitment is essentially an American-style put; the commitment buyer has the right to put his fixed-rate debt to the lender at a below-market rate if market rates exceed the maximum guaranteed by the commitment. Complicating this simple picture is the fact that the underlying security is a loan which has yet to be made, which will have the same time from drawdown to maturity no matter when the commitment is exercised. In a positive yield curve environment, term rates are expected to rise over time and hence the commitment is most likely to go into-the-money at the end of the commitment term. For this reason, the commitment is best modeled as a put on a forward security with a yield equal to the maximum rate, which will be delivered on the date the commitment expires.

Consider the simplified case of a six-month commitment to make a two-year bullet loan (all interest paid at maturity) of $1 million. The lending rate will be fixed on takedown at the lesser of 10% or the two-year Treasury rate plus 1%. The underlying security is a two-year, pure-discount security with a price of $1 million and a maturity value, at the 10% rate, of $1,210,000. The strike price, then, is $1 million. At present, the six-month Trea-

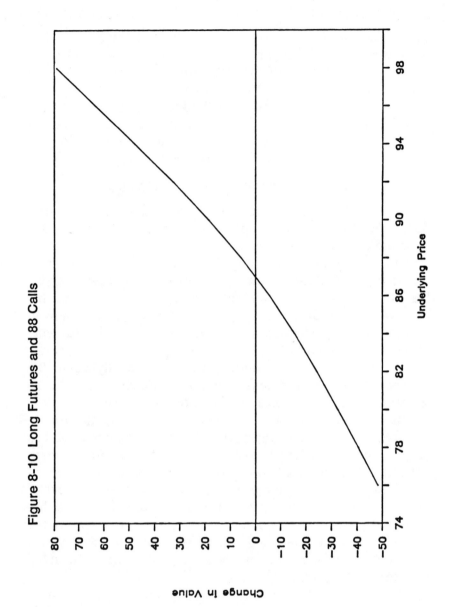

Figure 8-10 Long Futures and 88 Calls

sury yield is 6.50%, and the 2½-year Treasury yield is 7.50%. The forward rate from six months to 2½ years is thus 7.78 percent, and if market expectations are realized, the loan will be made at 8.78 percent. The price of the underlying security, then, is $1,210,000/ $(1.0878)^2$ = $1,022,556.

The volatility of the underlying security might be difficult to observe directly. However, if we observe the implied volatility of an exchange-traded option, we may be able to adjust it to derive a proxy for the implied volatility of the loan underlying the commitment. If we assume that rate volatility is constant for all maturities, we cannot observe the implied price volatility of, for example, ten-year note option and use it directly as the volatility of our two-year loan, since the longer duration of the ten-year note would make its price much more volatile than the value of our two-year security. To compensate, we must use Equation 8-3:

$$ V_1 = \frac{D_1}{D_2} \times \frac{(1 + r_2/2)}{(1 + r_1/2)} \times V_2 \qquad (8\text{-}3) $$

V_1 = proxy for volatility of security 1
D_1 = duration of security 1
r_1 = market rate for security 1 (semiannually compounded)
V_2 = observed implied volatility of an option on security 2
D_2 = duration of security 2 (semiannually compounded)
r_2 = market rate for security 2

In our example, V_1 is the volatility of the two-year loan underlying the commitment, D_1 = 2 and r_1 = .0878. V_2 is the implied volatility of a T-note futures option, for example, 12%; D_2 is the duration of the T-note futures computed as per Equation 1-9, for example, 6.5; and r_2 is the forward rate on the T-note futures, for example, 9.0%. Then,

$$ V_1 = \frac{2}{6.5} \times \frac{1.09}{1.0878} \times .12 = .037 $$

We now have all of the inputs required to evaluate the commitment as a put:

$$ U = 1,022,556 $$

$$S = 1,000,000$$

$$t = .5$$

$$r = .065$$

$$v = .037$$

$$h = 0$$

Plugging these inputs into the Black-Scholes put formulas, we arrive at an estimate of the value, delta, and gamma of the commitment:

$$\text{Value} = 2794.36$$

$$\text{Delta} = .19$$

$$\text{Gamma} = .10$$

We can compute the BPV of the underlying two-year loan:

$$\$1,022,556 \times .0001/1.0878 \times 2 = \$188.$$

The basis point value of the commitment, then, is

$$188 \times .19 = 35.72$$

and the change in BPV per basis point change in rate is

$$188 \times .10 = 18.80.$$

A cap on an adjustable rate loan is essentially a series of commitments on short-term forward securities. Consider the case of a 7½% cap on a $1 million one-year loan tied to 90-day LIBOR and adjusted quarterly. The cap might be analyzed as shown in Table 8-3a.

This analysis treats the cap as a call on three-month forward rates starting zero, three, six, and nine months out. As such, it uses the same methodology as used to evaluate a strip of options on Eurodollar futures.

There is an important difference between the cap and a strip of futures options, however; the cap pays off in arrears, when interest is due, rather than in advance, as do Eurodollar futures. Compensation for this can be made by present-valuing the BPVs of the forward securities to reflect the in-arrears interest pay-

Table 8-3a 7½% Cap as a Sequence of Options
(Rate Volatility = 19.6%; short-term rate set to 6.5%)

Underlying Maturity	LIBOR	3 Month Forward LIBOR	Rate-Based Call Price (%)	Delta	Gamma
3 Mo.	7.00	7.00	.098833	.25	.47
6 Mo.	7.24	7.35	.217422	.43	.55
9 Mo.	7.38	7.39	.235069	.45	.55
12 Mo.	7.50	7.45	.263160	.48	.55

ments, and using these adjusted BPVs to calculate a dollar value, BPV, and ΔBPV for the options, as in Table 8-3b.

A collar is a commitment or cap which is partially or totally paid for by a floor rate accepted by the cap buyer. The buyer in essence accepts a minimum rate in exchange for a cap on the maximum rate he will have to pay during the life of the collar. In essence the collar buyer buys a put on price (or a call on rates) at a price below the current market and sells a call on price (or a put

Table 8-3b 7½% Cap Value, BPV, and ΔBPV

Underlying Maturity	Adjusted Underlying BPV[1]	$ Call Price[2]	Add-On BPV[3]	Add-On ΔBPV[4]
3 Mo.	24.57	242.83	6.14	.12
6 Mo.	24.55	533.77	10.56	.13
9 Mo.	24.55	577.09	11.05	.14
12 Mo.	24.54	645.79	11.77	.14
Total for Cap		$1,999.48	$39.52	$.53

[1]Change in underlying price for one basis point change in the add-on rate, discounted by forward rate to reflect payment in arrears.

[2]BPV times rate-based call price in basis points.

[3]Underlying BPV times call delta; equals change in call values per basis point chante in add-on rates.

[4]Underlying BPV times call gamma divided by 100 (gamma on Table 8-3a reflects change in delta per whole percent rate change; divide by 100 to get gamma per basis point); equals change in calls' add-on BPV per basis point change in add-on rates.

on rates) at a price level above the current market, as illustrated in Figure 8-11.

Evaluation of a collar consists of a separate evaluation of the cap or commitment portion and of the floor portion. Collars are often touted as *no-cost collars* and are offered for no fee to prospective buyers. In reality, these collars are *no-cost* in the same sense that a casino requires no cover charge of its customers. The zero and double-zero spaces on the roulette wheel ensure that the house will extract a small profit over time even from players who bet both red and black on every spin. In the case of the collar, the cap is set further away from the market price than the floor, ensuring that the vendor can lay off the risk at a small profit. Collars may nonetheless prove worthwhile to buyers if they offer better control of buyers' specific rate risk than other alternatives.

Modeling Very Long-Term Options

An obvious inconsistency arises in applying the Black-Scholes model to options on fixed-income securities and futures. The model at once assumes that the value of these securities fluctuates due to changing rates, and that short-term financing rates are constant. Fortunately, the model's results are relatively insensitive to assumptions about short-term rates when time to expiration is short—for example, less than one year. When modeling longer-term options such as a three-year commitment, assumed financing costs become increasingly important and hinder the use of the Black-Scholes formula.

Conclusion

The range of risks that can be evaluated and controlled using option theory and exchange traded options, is large and expanding. The assumptions behind the Black-Scholes model are often violated by the markets, and the option components in some risk management situations are occasionally more complex than can be analyzed accurately using the basic Black-Scholes formula. Nonetheless, by using the formula as a rule of thumb and, more importantly, using option concepts to guide the analysis of risk management problems, risk managers will be able to develop strategies which will substantially mitigate risks which they would otherwise have to accept.

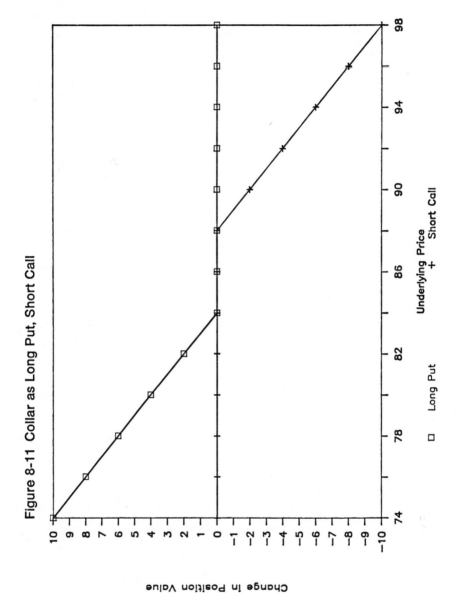

Figure 8-11 Collar as Long Put, Short Call

Rate Behavior and Rate Calculation Methods

Yield Curve Behavior

Arbitrage activity ensures that certain relationships will prevail between market yields on securities with differing maturities. Consider a market in which yields rise linearly from 5% for three-month securities to 10% for three-year securities. All market participants believe that this structure of term rates—or *yield curve*—will not change over time. Rational market participants will quickly conclude that they can issue three-month securities at 5% and use the proceeds to fund the purchase of three-year assets yielding 10%, earning a 5% profit spread. By acting on this conclusion, they will drive the price of three-month securities down and the price of three-year securities up, until it is impossible to earn a profit spread by so doing.

A positively sloped yield curve thus will not persist unless market participants expect short-term rates to rise over time. If market participants are certain that short-term rates will rise over time, a rising yield curve can persist. The market participant who contemplates issuing a series of three-month securities to fund a three-year asset will observe expected three-month rates over the next three years and tally the total interest expense from issuing a sequence of twelve consecutive three-month securities. He or she will then compare this expense to the total return on the three-year asset. If the expense of funding equals the total return, he or she will not act, and the term structure of rates will remain in equilibrium.

In equilibrium, when future or forward short-term rates are known with certainty,

$$(1 + {}_0r_{.25})^{.25} \times (1 + {}_{.25}r_{.5})^{.25} \times \cdots \times (1 + {}_{2.75}r_3)^{.25} = (1 + {}_0r_3)^3$$

where ${}_0r_{25}$ equals the current three-month rate, ${}_{.25}r_5$ equals the forward rate on a three-month security issued three months hence, etc., and ${}_0r_3$ is the market rate on a current three-year security.

If market participants admit the possibility of unanticipated changes in the yield curve, this scenario is complicated considerably. Consider a market in which the yield curve is flat at 10% for all maturities. No specific change in short-term rates is anticipated over time, but market participants think that random events over time may shift the yield curve up or down without warning. A market participant might then trade as follows:

1. Buy a three month, pure discount security for $1 million.

$$F = 1,000,000 \times 1.10^{.25} = 1,024,113.69$$
$$BPV = 1,000,000 \times .0001/1.10 \times .25 = 22.73$$

2. By a ten-year, pure discount security for $1 million.

$$F = 1,000,000 \times 1.10^{10} = 2,593,742.46$$
$$BPV = 1,000,000 \times .0001/1.10 \times 10 = 909.09$$

3. Sell a 5.125 year, pure discount security for $2 million.

$$F = 2,000,000 \times 1.10^{5.125} = 3,259.624.00$$
$$BPV = 2,000,000 \times .0001/1.10 \times 5.125 = 931.82$$

The market participant has a position which has a BPV of zero and which neither makes nor loses money. Yet, consider the effect of a 5% drop in the level of the yield curve. The change in present value of the securities will result in a gain in market value.

3-month asset:	$P = 1,024,113.69/1.05^{.25} =$	1,011,697.90
10-year asset:	$P = 2,593,742.46/1.05^{10} =$	1,592,332.87
5.125-year liability:	$P = 3,259,624.00/1.05^{5.125} =$	$-2,538,471.83$
	Gain in Market Value	65,558.95

In the event of a 5% increase in the level of the yield curve, the market participant will also experience a gain:

3-month asset:	$P = 1,024,113.69/1.15^{.25} =$		988,948.58
10-year asset:	$P = 2,593,742.46/1.15^{10} =$		641,133.47
5.125-year liability:	$P = 3,259,624.00/1.15^{5.125} =$	$-$	1,592,542.66
	Gain in Market Value		37,539.39

By establishing his or her position, the market participant has created a free option which will pay off if the level of the yield curve shifts up or down. The value of this option is a function of the anticipated volatility of market rates. As numerous market participants catch on to this strategy, they will bid up the price of short- and long-term securities, and sell down the price of medium-term securities. As a result, the yield curve will not be flat, but concave from below, even though market participants' current average expectations are that short-term rates will not change over time.

Rate Calculation Methods

Implicit in the word *rate* is the assumption that it is a measure of return over time. Typically rates are quoted on an annualized basis.

As seen in Chapter 1, the correct relationship between annualized rate, price, maturity value, and time for a security which *compounds* or reinvests, interest once per period is:

$$P = \frac{F}{(1 + r)^N} \qquad\qquad (1\text{-}2a)$$

or

$$r = (F/P)^{1/N} - 1 \qquad\qquad (1\text{-}2b)$$

where
   F = Face value
   P = Price
   r = Rate of interest per period
   N = Number of periods to maturity

To calculate a simple return (interest not reinvested at any point) of r per period over N periods, we assume that N times the annual rate is earned over one period.

$$P = \frac{F}{1 + r \times N} \qquad \text{(A1-1)}$$

so that

$$r = (F/P - 1) \times 1/N \qquad \text{(A1-2)}$$

To calculate a return compounded more often than one time per period, say X times per period, the return per compounding period equals r/X and the number of compounding periods equals $N \times X$. The rate r compounded X times per period is

$$P = \frac{F}{(1 + r/X)^{[N \times X]}} \qquad \text{(A1-3)}$$

and so

$$r = [(F/P)^{(1/[N \times X])} - 1] \times X \qquad \text{(A1-4)}$$

In the extreme case, where compounding occurs an infinite number of times per period (continuous compounding), the relationship becomes

$$P = F \times e^{(-r \times n)} \qquad \text{(A1-5)}$$

or

$$r = \frac{\ln (F/P)}{N} \qquad \text{(A1-6)}$$

where
  r = Continuously compounded rate of return per period
  e = Natural log base, 2.718281828
  $\ln$ = Natural log; $\ln [e^{(r \times N)}] = r \times N$

The r calculated for any number of compoundings per period can be translated precisely into the r calculated for any other number of compoundings per period by the following formula:

$$R_1 = X_1 \times [(1 + r_2/X_2)^{(X2/X1)} - 1] \qquad \text{(A1-7)}$$

Translation from continuous compounding to compounding once per period is calculated by the following formula:

$$r_{\text{annual}} = e^{r\text{comp.}} - 1 \qquad \text{(A1-8)}$$

This direct relationship between rates based on different compounding periods makes irrelevant the compounding assumptions used in calculating the r of a security; any number of compoundings X will result in an exact description of the change in value of the security over time. What is important is that:

The compounding method must be known for every r;

and

Any two rs being compared should be calculated using the same compounding method.

If two rs with different compounding methods must be compared, translation from one compounding period to another is easily accomplished using Equations A1-7 and A1-8.

Electronic calculators with yield to maturity or internal rate of return functions typically assume that compounding occurs whenever cash flows occur. For a bond with semiannual coupon, maturing in N years, this means that YTM is calculated so that

$$P = \frac{C_1}{(1 + r/2)^1} + \frac{C_2}{(1 + r/2)^2} + \frac{C_3}{(1 + r/3)^3} + \cdots$$
$$+ \frac{C_N + M}{(1 + r)^{2 \times N}}$$

This is a semiannually compounded representation of the YTM. The annually compounded YTM would be

$$P = \frac{C_1}{(1 + r)^{.5}} + \frac{C_2}{(1 + r)^1} + \frac{C_3}{(1 + r)^{1.5}} + \cdots + \frac{C_N + M}{(1 + r)^N}$$

Be sure you know what compounding period is implicit in your calculator-derived yields to maturity.

The compounding assumptions you imply will have implications for measurement of yield curve behavior.

A flat yield curve based on one compounding assumption will translate into a flat yield curve (albeit at a different level) based on any other compounding assumption. However, translating between compounding assumptions when the curve has slope or curvature will change the slope and curvature of the curve, as illustrated in Figure A-1.

When the initial yield curve is not flat, what constitutes a parallel shift depends on your compounding assumptions.

Figure A-1

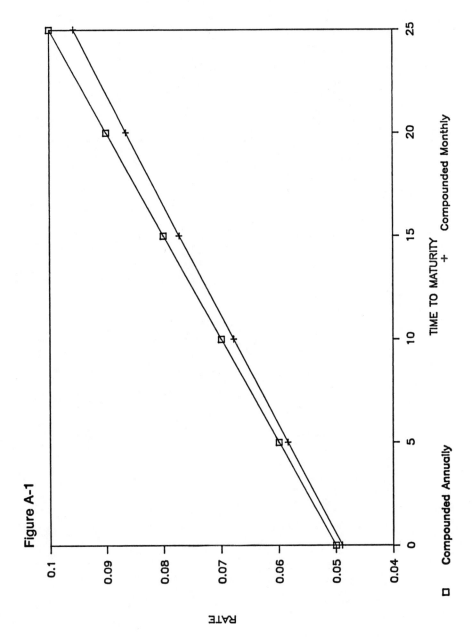

□ Compounded Annually
+ Compounded Monthly

Trading Mechanics and Strategy

All futures exchanges are regulated by the Commodity Futures Trading Commission (CFTC). The CFTC approves the establishment of new U.S. futures exchanges, approves exchange procedures and new contract introductions, and enforces commodity law. An industry self-regulatory group, the National Futures Association, establishes and enforces rules concerning professional qualifications and industry conduct.

The exchanges themselves perform numerous basic functions. They provide a physical location for trading; they determine who is allowed to buy and sell on the exchanges; they govern which contracts will be traded and trading hours; they back the integrity of the trades; they report trade prices to the public; they arbitrate disputes, and, through a clearing subsidiary or division, they coordinate the matching and recording of trades, the administration of margin accounts, etc.

Membership

Membership to an exchange is restricted to a certain number of *seats* which are bought and sold like any other commodity. To receive a membership, one must buy a seat and have a personal (or corporate) history free from evidence of misconduct. To actively trade, one must first go through a relatively brief exchange-provided training program covering trading conduct and exchange procedures and then demonstrate the financial wherewithal to meet the obligations assumed in trading. Any legal person, corporate as well as individual, may buy a seat. The buyer, or the buyer's agent, may trade. Seats may also be leased to individuals or firms wishing to trade but not to own a seat.

The Trading Floor

The physical trading floor contains several trading *pits* or *rings,* octagonal in shape and consisting of concentric steps rising from the exchange floor, then descending into the center of the pit. On some exchanges (for example, the Chicago Board of Trade), a raised pulpit is positioned at the edge of the pit, from which exchange personnel monitor trading and enter observed trade prices into a computer terminal for reporting and public dissemination. On other exchanges (for example, the Chicago Mercantile Exchange), pulpits have been replaced by exchange personnel who stand in the pits and relay price data for computer input by walkie-talkie.

Generally, a particular type of contract is traded in its own trading pit. Different delivery months of a given contract are traded in specific sections of the pit. For example, the first contract to be delivered may be traded on a substantial portion of the pit's perimeter, the following contract may be traded in the center of the pit, and back months may be traded in the remaining perimeter area.

Along the walls of the trading floor are rows of desks which contain telephone banks, cash market quote screens, time stamps, file racks, and other paraphernalia which allow information and outside orders to be transmitted to the floor. Above the desks on the walls are price boards on which trade information is displayed, including the opening trading range, daily high and low trade prices, the last three prices traded, the previous day's closing price, and exchange-imposed price limits (if any). Diagrams of the Board of Trade and Mercantile Exchange trading floors are provided in Figures A2-1 and A2-2.

The denizens of the pit include members, who are empowered to buy and sell futures or options, and their support staffs. There are two broad classes of members—*brokers* and *locals.* Brokers do not ever trade to earn a speculative profit for their own accounts; they execute trades on behalf of their customers in exchange for a small fee per contract. Brokers may be

Figure A2-1 The Chicago Board of Trade
Financial Futures Trading Floor

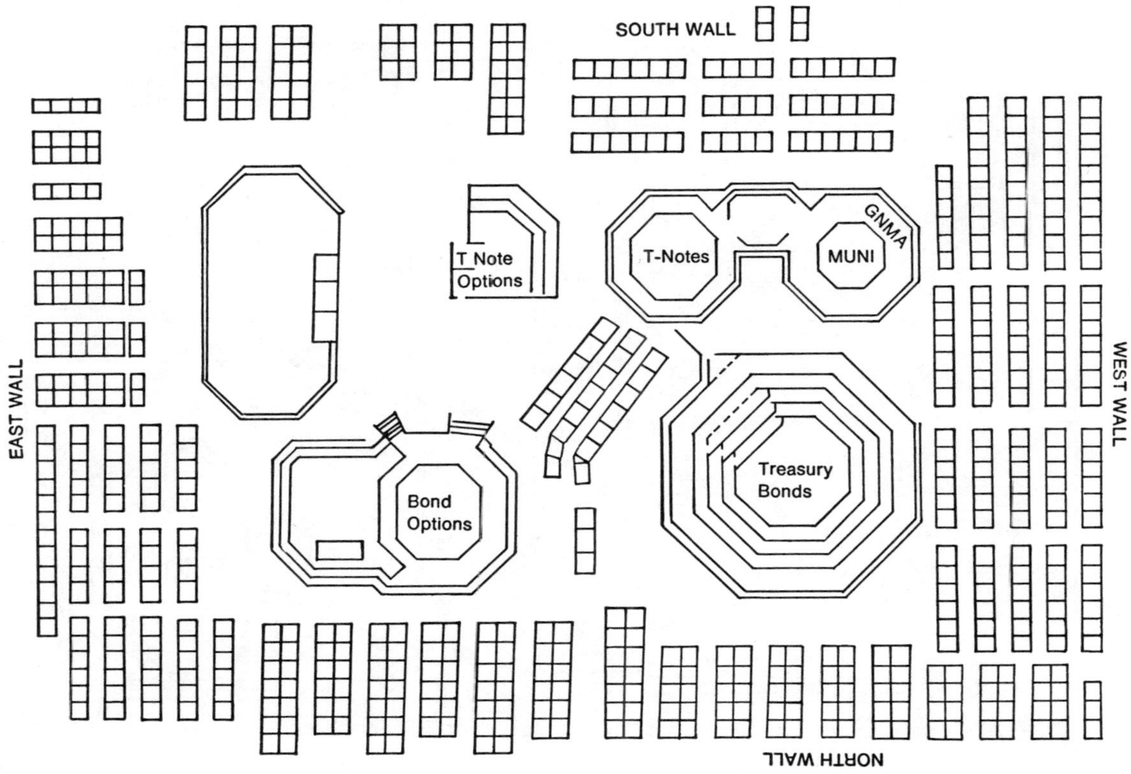

WEST WALL

NORTH WALL

SOUTH WALL

GNMA

MUNI

T-Notes

Treasury Bonds

T Note Options

Bond Options

EAST WALL

Figure A2-2 The Chicago Mercantile Exchange Center

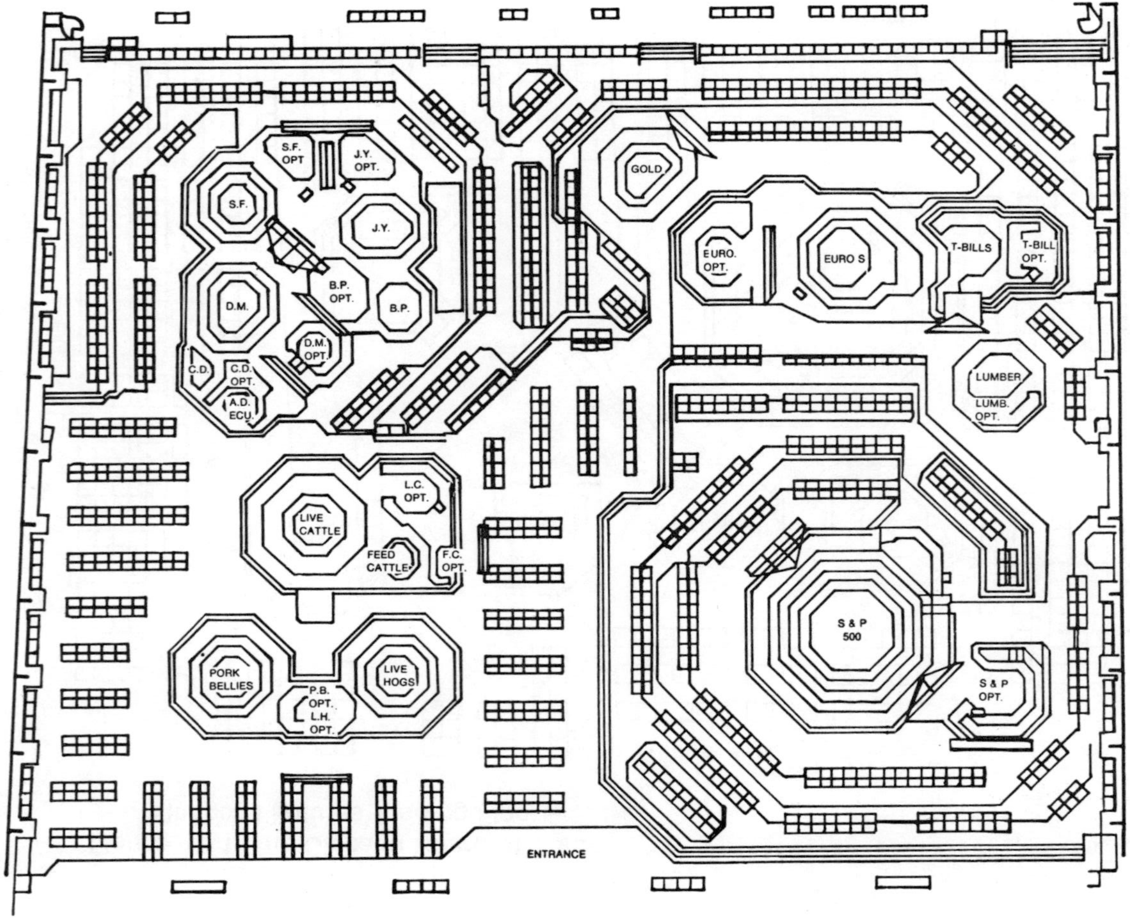

firm brokers who execute solely on behalf of the customer of their firms, or *independent floor brokers,* who are individuals who execute on behalf of individuals or firms who are their clients.

Locals, on the other hand, are members who buy and sell futures only to earn a speculative profit for themselves. Three trading styles predominate among locals. *Scalpers* assume large positions for short periods of time and attempt to offset their positions quickly for a profit of a tick or two. *Day traders* assume (usually) somewhat smaller positions but hold them for a period of hours, to profit from larger, longer-term changes in market directions. *Position-takers* may hold positions for days or weeks to profit from very long-term moves in market price.

Brokers and locals have a symbiotic relationship. Were trading restricted to brokers, a broker with an order, for example, to sell 500 contracts at price X would have to wait until other brokers received orders to buy a total of 500 at X before filling the order. The local population acts as a reservoir of liquidity, buying from one broker at X and holding their positions until order flows come in from other brokers to buy (hopefully, from the local's point of view, at a price higher than X).

The Order Cycle

An institutional futures user will typically transact as the customer of a futures brokerage firm. Suppose a customer needs to sell 500 March T-bond futures. He will call his broker and ask for a price quote. The broker may reply, "The market is 99-16 bid, 99-17 offered, 100 by 50," or simply, "six bid at seven, one hundred by fifty." The latter quote assumes that the customer is aware that the full price is between 99-10 and 99-20. If the customer does not know where the price is, he might ask, "What's the handle?"— which means "What is the full price bid and offered?" The custom of quoting the last digit of a futures price arises because the floor population communicates largely by means of hand signals, and there are only ten fingers on the human hand. The qualifier "100 by 50" is an indication that the broker believes that there are bidders to buy up to 100 contracts at 99-10, and offerors to sell up to 50 contracts at 99-17. She might specify further that the bids or offers are *on paper*—believed to be written customer orders that floor brokers are obligated to fill if possible—or local—bids or offers by locals who may retract them quickly.

The customer may place several types of orders, as described in Table A2-1. Only one type of order assures the customer of selling 500 contracts immediately at the best available price—the *market order.* If the customer directs his broker to "sell 500 March bonds at the market," the floor broker executing the trade will sell 500 contracts immediately at the best available price. The quantity sold is assured, but the price is not. Other order types are *limit orders,* specifying the minimum price at which the contracts may be sold. On a limit order, the contracts traded will be at the limit price or better, but there is no assurance that the floor broker will be able to sell all 500 contracts at the limit price or better.

If the customer places a market order or a limit order between the current bid or offer, chances are the order will be transmitted verbally, i.e., by hand-signal, to the floor broker in the pit. A phone clerk at the brokerage's desk will indicate via hand signal to a clerk supporting the floor broker to "sell 500 at (the market or the limit price)." A buy order will be transmitted with a signal to "pay (market or limit price) for 500 contracts." (Illustrations of the hand signals are shown in Figure A2-3.) The clerk supporting the floor broker will tell the floor broker the order. The floor broker will look at other traders in the pit to see what bids are available. If the order is to sell at the market, the floor broker may shout an offer of 7 and signal the price with both hands, indicating the offer is on a quantity of more than five contracts. An eager bidder may ask, "What size?" The broker must exercise judgment; revealing a large offer may scare off local bidders, whereas revealing too small a size may result in selling less than the bidder is willing to buy. Attracting no more bidders, the broker immediately "hits 6 bids," i.e., all bidders—local or broker—at a price of 96-16 until all 500 contracts are sold, or until no more 6- bidders are seen in the pit. In the latter case, the broker may have to search for bids at 96-15 or below to sell the unfilled balance of the order.

The broker, while filling the order, writes the transaction down on a small card, including the identity of the buyer, the number of contracts they buy, the price at which they bought,

Table A2-1 Order Types

Market	Buy or sell a specified number of contracts at the best available price. Execution is assured but not price.
Limit	Buy or sell a specified number of contracts at a specified price or better. Price is assured but not execution.
MIT	*Market if touched* orders are like limit orders in that they specify a price. However, once the price is touched, the MIT becomes a market order, assuring execution.
Stop	Buy or sell when the market reaches a specified price. Used to limit losses or initiate a new position. Becomes a market order when the price of the stop is elected. A buy stop is placed above the current market. A sell stop is placed below the current market. Execution is assured but cannot guarantee a predetermined dollar price.
Stop Limit	A more defined type of stop order. Whereas stop orders become market orders at a specified price, stop limit indicates a price limit after the specified price has been touched. However, in an extreme market this order does not assure execution.
MOC	*Market on close* can be filled as a market order only during the closing range.
FOK	*Fill or kill* instructs the broker to bid or offer an order several times at a specified price. If it cannot be filled, it is immediately killed (canceled).
OCO	*One cancels the other* involves two orders and two separate order forms. Execution of one order automatically cancels the other. Typically, one will buy a buy (sell) price order, and the other will be a stop order.
Spread	Indicates the simultaneous taking of long and short positions, profiting from the change in the price differential.

and the time of the transactions. Complementary data is recorded by the buyer on the other side of the trade. Later, the broker's clearing firm will match buys and sells from information taken from the associated trade cards.

While the floor broker is executing the trade, the brokerage phone clerk is writing information about the trade (customer ac-

Figure A2-3 Part I.

a. Buy

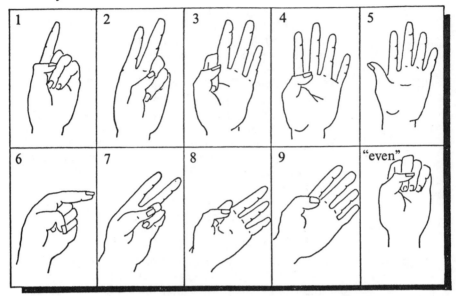

b. Sell

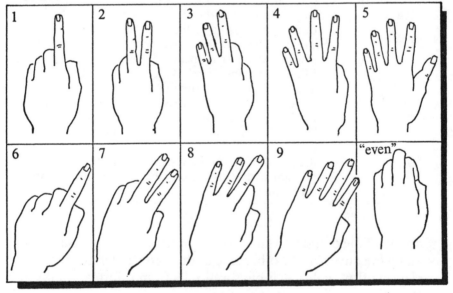

Figure A2-3 Part II.

a. Pay PRICE for QUANTITY.

"Pay five on twenty."

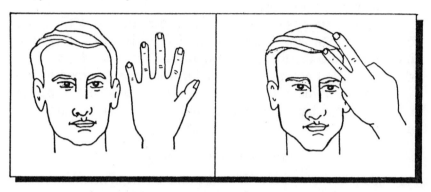

b. Sell QUANTITY for PRICE.

"Sell sixty-two at even."

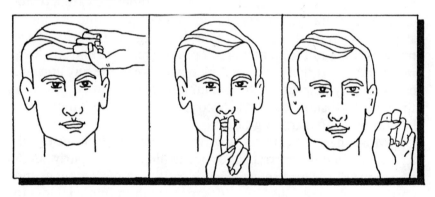

Quantity is by the face; price is away from the face. For quantity, tens are on the forehead, ones on the chin.

count number, contract, quantity, and order price) on an order form. On an order flashed into the pit by hand signal, the clerk may write "V" to indicate that the order slip relates to an order previously entered verbally.

She time stamps the order and has a runner walk the order form up to the broker's clerk. The clerk records prices and quantities filled onto the form, and the runner returns it to the desk where the filled completed order form is time stamped again. Later, the customer's brokerage firm will record the trade for reports to the customer using information taken from the order form.

The Clearing Process

All traders in the pit are affiliated with a clearing member of the exchange, a firm which undertakes to record the trade and to ensure that the information on every purchase transaction exactly complements the information of the corresponding sale transaction(s). This matching procedure is done with information taken from the trader's trade card. If all information matches the buy and sell cards for a particular trade, the trade is cleared, or recorded in exchange records. From that point on, the exchange steps between the buyer and seller, backing the integrity of the trade with the full faith and credit of the exchange and its clearing members. If there is a discrepancy between the buy and sell cards in any respect, such as counterparty, quantity, price, or time of transaction, the trade becomes an *out-trade,* which must be corrected after trading hours.

Most out-trades are easily corrected, occurring because of illegibility, time-discrepancies or miscopied counterparty identification. Buyer and seller meet, identify the discrepancy, and correct it. More serious out-trades may result in financial loss to one or both of the traders involved. These might include price discrepancies, for example, where a buyer believes he bought at 96-16, and the seller believes he sold at 96-17); quantity discrepancies, where the buyer believes he bought 40 contracts, and seller believes he sold 50; *don't knows* (DKs), where the buyer or seller disavows knowledge that the trade occurred; or *buy versus buy* and *sell versus sell,* where the buyer and seller both believe that they bought, or both believe that they sold. The custom is for buyer and seller to split the difference when financial loss is incurred. If they are unable to agree on a way to remedy the out-trade, they may take the trade to binding arbitration. The arbitrator, an exchange official, usually instructs the traders to split the difference. Traders usually shun other traders who are believed to be involved in unusually large numbers of out-trades.

Margin

The exchange establishes minimum levels of funds which must be maintained in the margin accounts of parties having futures positions. These required margin levels may be changed by the exchange to reflect changes in price volatility. Generally, exchanges set two margin levels, an *initial margin,* which must be posted when a new position is established and a *maintenance margin* level, below which margin balances may not fall for existing futures positions. Different margin levels may be established for speculative and hedging positions, or for spread trades and outright positions, reflecting differences in the degree of risk associated with trades for different purposes or with different combinations of positions. Required initial and maintenance margins are quoted on a per contract or per spread basis.

At the end of trading each day, all futures positions are marked to market and the change in price for that day is added to or subtracted from the position holder's margin account.

Maintenance margins were developed as a way to reduce the number of money transfers required to keep margin accounts at acceptable levels. The balance in a margin account may fall below the initial margin level, but as long as it is above the maintenance margin level, the position holder will not be required to deposit additional funds. If the margin account balance falls below the maintenance level, a margin call is issued, requiring the position holder to bring his margin account balance back to the initial margin level. Conversely, if the margin account balances rise, the position holder is free to withdraw the excess above the initial margin level.

Margin is a performance bond, not an initial investment, and remains the property of the position holder. In lieu of cash, the position holder may post Treasury securities with two years or less to maturity into his margin account. Ninety percent of the value of bills posted and a smaller percent of the value of notes posted is counted toward meeting margin requirements. Posted margin cash and securities are held in a segregated account by the futures brokerage firm on behalf of the position holder.

What to Expect from a Broker

When a broker quotes a market, for example, "99-16 bid, 99-17 offered, 100 by 50," the customer may reasonably expect that with an immediate order she can sell 100 contracts at 99-16, or buy 50 contracts at 99-17. If the quote is "6 bid at 7, all local," the customer can expect to buy or sell only a small, uncertain quantity at the bid or offer. On a market order, the customer may expect to be filled at prices within the range of prices traded at the time she placed the order.

If the customer feels her fill may have been done at unfair prices, she may obtain a time and price study from the exchange, listing the prices at which trades occurred when her trade was executed. It is illegal for a broker to *race trades*—to initiate a purchase for his own account before a standing buy order is executed for a customer. Conversely, it is also illegal for a broker to *bucket* an order—match buys and sells of two different customers off the exchange floor—even when this might result in a better fill for both customers.

When a broker reports a fill to the customer, he must absorb the loss if the actual execution is not done at as favorable a price due to error in execution or reporting.

A market order should be filled as quickly as possible and a fill reported in at most a couple of minutes from the time the order is placed. Prices obtained on a market order may take longer to report due to pit congestion, or the need to fill other orders before completed order forms are retrieved. Limit orders may take hours to fill, or may not be filled if market prices do not permit. The fact that a quote screen indicates that a trade was done at a limit price does not mean that a limit order should have been completely or partially filled. The customer may have a standing order to sell 500 at 96-17; but a print at 96-17 may simply mean that a local sold a single contract to another local at that price and there was no real opportunity to fill the customer's order. If a price prints which is better than the price on a limit order, however, it suggests that the limit order should have been completely filled.

Execution Strategy

Often the best strategy for an institutional customer to take is to hit the available bid or to lift or take the available offer, or to buy or sell at the market. Occasionally, better execution can be achieved by working the order in various ways:

- A seller sees that the size is 500 bid, 50 offered. The bid size is increasing. He may be able to get the edge by joining the offer or by waiting a moment to see if the price rises. Locals, seeing the larger bid, may step in front of the bid.

- Showing large size in a local market may scare the locals, causing their bids and offers to move unfavorably. It may be better when trading is quiet in a liquid market to place several smaller orders in succession to achieve the desired position. The risk in this strategy is that the release of news or a large order from someone else may move the market against the customer. In markets characterized by few floor participants, this strategy may not work well.

Technical Analysis

Traders in the pits are the last people to hear fundamental news affecting their markets. Instead, they must rely on observed order flow, expressions of fear or greed on other traders' faces, and their knowledge of what prices have recently elicited trading by floor brokers (indicating, perhaps, at what prices active limit orders may lie or where stop-loss orders may be triggered). A principal tool applied by traders to keep track of the latter is *technical analysis,* the study of past price behavior to predict future price behavior. The usefulness of technical trading is hotly disputed by academics. Nonetheless, because it is used and discussed so widely, a basic explanation of technical analysis may prove useful.

Two principal methods are used to display price histories for technical analysis: the bar chart and the point-and-figure chart. The axes of a bar chart are price (on the vertical) and time (on the horizontal). Within each time period, the high and low price traded are connected by a line (or bar), and the last price traded during the period is displayed as a hatch-mark somewhere on the bar, as illustrated in Figure A2-4.

A basic use of the bar chart is to attempt to determine where resistance and support levels may be (i.e., price levels where selling or buying activity have been elicited in the past). These levels are determined by drawing lines between the extreme highs or lows attained over some length of time. A related concept is the *trading channel*. When the market highs reach successively higher levels over time and lows also halt at successively higher levels, a line connecting highs and another line connecting lows describes a *bull channel* in which trading appears to occur. The inference drawn from this analysis is that trading will continue to be contained in the channel, and thus that prices will trend upward.

Another type of analysis applied to bar charts is the use of moving averages of highs, lows, and last traded prices. Typically, shorter- and longer-term moving averages are calculated; when the shorter-term moving average crosses the longer moving averages, a break-out is considered likely in the direction of the shorter moving average price change.

Point-and-figure charts depict price on the vertical axis and number of large price reversals on the horizontal axis. An example of a "1 × 3" point-and-figure chart is provided in Figure A2-5. Large price moves in one direction are drawn in a single column of the chart, regardless of the time taken for the move to occur. Up moves are depicted with Xs and down moves with Os. Small reversals in price movement (less than three ticks) are depicted in the same column. If a move of three or more ticks occurs, a new column is started one column to the right. The resulting patterns are subjected to support and resistance, trend-line and channel analysis in a fashion similar to that used on bar charts.

In addition, certain formations can occur which are considered significant:

Figure A2-4 A Bar Chart Used in Technical Analysis

MAR IMM EURO$ thru 02/17/87

(High—Low—Close)

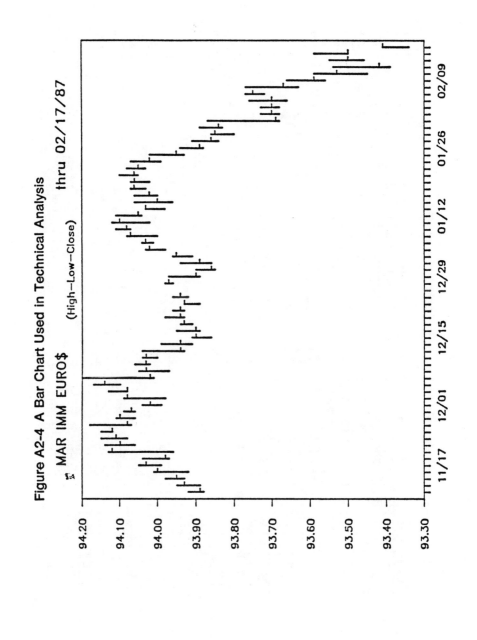

Figure A2-5 Point-and-Figure Chart Used in Technical Analysis

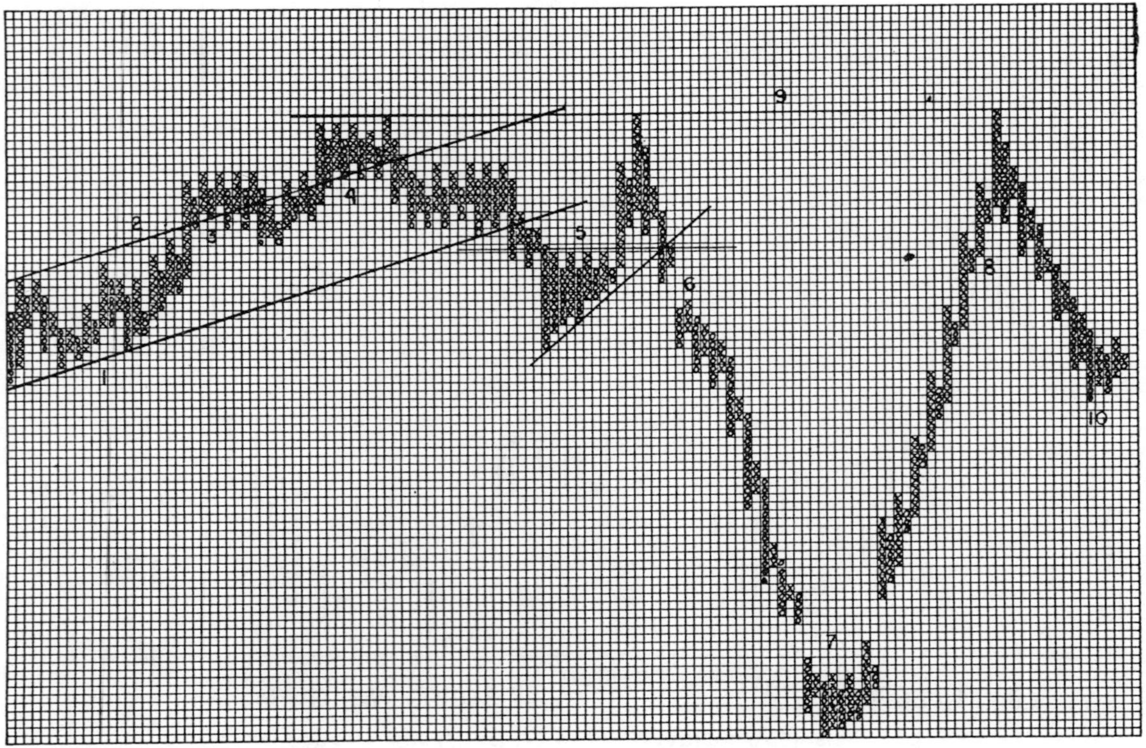

- *Gaps* in the chart which occur when prices jump several ticks at once are said to indicate attractive levels for prices to settle in later trading. If the price gaps from 95 to 95-16 on the way up to 100, chartists anticipate that the market will try to fill the gap, dropping to 95 in continuous trading, on some future date. An *island reversal* occurs when prices gap upward, plateau for a short while, and then gap downward. This is regarded as an indicator of a tired bull market and of further price declines ahead. An *exhaustion gap* is an upward gap at the end of a strong bull market. Exhaustion gaps are said to represent tired markets, inclined to reverse direction after a long rally or protracted decline.

- *Ascending-* or *descending-pennant* formations occur when the chart depicts a triangle (or pennant) pointing up or down. This is said to augur an eventual market break-out in the direction to which the pennant points.

- *Head and shoulder* formations are similar in concept to an exhaustion gap. The market rises, plateaus, rises, falls, and plateaus, creating a shape which looks like the outline of a head and shoulders, and auguring a decline in the market when the right shoulder is traced. An inverted head and shoulders is said to foreshadow a rally.

- *Triple tops* or *triple bottoms* are said to reveal particularly stubborn resistance or support levels through which the market cannot penetrate. Failing to penetrate, the market will then be more likely to back away from the area of resistance.

Summary of Formulas

Variable Names Used in Chapter 1

P	Current market *Price*
F	*Face* or *Final* maturity value
r	*Rate* of return
N	*Number* of years to maturity
$\ln(x)$	The *Natural Log* of x; if $x = e^y$, then $\ln(x) = y$, where e equals the natural log base, 2.718281828.
Δ	"Delta", the greek letter d. Before another variable name, denotes a change in the value of that variable.
D	*Duration*
BPV	*Basis Point Value*
SPV	*Slope Point Value*
M	Amount due at *Maturity*
PV	*Present Value*
YTM	*Yield To Maturity*
IRR	*Internal Rate of Return*

$$P = \frac{F}{(1 + r)} \qquad (1\text{-}1)$$

$$P = \frac{F}{(1 + r)^N}. \qquad (1\text{-}2\text{a})$$

$$F = P \times (1 + r)^N \qquad (1\text{-}2\text{b})$$

$$r = (F/P)^{(1/N)} - 1 \qquad (1\text{-}2\text{c})$$

213

$$N = \frac{\ln (F/P)}{\ln (1 + r)}. \tag{1-2d}$$

$$\frac{\Delta r}{(1 + r)} \times D = - \frac{\Delta P}{P}. \tag{1-3}$$

$$D = N. \tag{1-4}$$

$$\text{BPV} = -P \times \frac{.0001}{(1 + r)} \times D \tag{1-5}$$

$$\text{BPV} = \frac{F}{(1 + r - .00005)^N} - \frac{F}{(1 + r + .00005)^N}. \tag{1-6}$$

$$\text{Portfolio BPV} = \text{BPV}_1 + \text{BPV}_2 + \cdots + \text{BPV}_P \tag{1-7}$$

$$D = \frac{(P_1 \times N_1) + (P_2 \times N_2) + \cdots + (P_P \times N_P)}{P_1 + P_2 + P_3 + \cdots + P_P} \tag{1-8}$$

$$D = \frac{\text{BPV}}{P} \times \frac{1 + r}{.0001} \tag{1-9}$$

$$P = \frac{C_1}{(1 + r)^1} + \frac{C_2}{(1 + r)^2} + \cdots + \frac{C_N + M}{(1 + r)^N} \tag{1-10}$$

Variable Names Used in Chapter 2

r_x	Rate for the term denoted by the subscript
AP	Arbitrage Profit
FP	Futures Price
CP	Cash Price
n	Number of days to maturity
BERR	Break Even Repo Rate
FFP	Fair Futures Price
Basis	Difference between futures invoice price and deliverable cash dollar price
T	Time in years until a hedged event occurs
X	A quantity of securities

$$AP = FP - [CP \times (1 + r \times n/360)] \tag{2-1}$$

$$BERR = \frac{FP - CP}{CP} \times \frac{360}{n} \tag{2-2}$$

$$FFP = CP \times [1 + (r \times n/360)] \tag{2-3}$$

$$Basis = FP - CP. \tag{2-4}$$

$$Basis = FP - CP = CP \times r \times n/360. \qquad (2\text{-}5)$$

Variable Names Used in Chapter 3

AI	Accrued Coupon *I*ncome as of date a cash note or bond is purchased.
C	*C*oupon
DP	*D*ays *P*assed since last coupon payment
TD	*T*otal *D*ays between last coupon and next
r_a	Add-on *R*ate
M	*M*aturity value of an add-on security
I	*I*nitial price or face value of an add-on security
n	*N*umber of days to maturity
d	*D*iscount on a Treasury bill
F	*F*ace value of a Treasury security
P	Current *P*rice of a security
BEY	*B*ond *E*quivalent *Y*ield
BPV	*B*asis *P*oint *V*alue
$BERR$	*B*reak *E*ven *R*epo *R*ate
CF	*C*onversion *F*actor
M	Years from delivery to *M*aturity (for conversion factors)

$$\text{Dollar Price} = \text{face value} \times \frac{\%\ \text{of Par Price}}{100} + \text{Coupon Accrual.}$$
$$(3\text{-}1)$$

$$AI = .5 \times C \times \frac{DP}{TD} \qquad (3\text{-}2)$$

$$r_a = (M/I - 1) \times 360/n \qquad (3\text{-}3)$$

$$M = I \times (I + r_a \times n/360). \qquad (3\text{-}4)$$

$$I' = I\frac{360 + r_a \times n}{360 + r_a' \times n'} \qquad (3\text{-}5)$$

$$d = (F - P)/F \times 360/n \qquad (3\text{-}6)$$

$$P = F \times [1 - d \times n/360]. \qquad (3\text{-}7)$$

$$r_a = \frac{360}{n} \times \left(\frac{1}{1 - d \times n/360} - 1\right). \qquad (3\text{-}8)$$

$$BEY = \frac{d \times 365/360}{1 - d \times n/360}. \qquad \text{(3-9)}$$

$$r = \left(\frac{1}{1 - d \times n/360}\right)^{(365/n)} - 1. \qquad \text{(3-10)}$$

$$r = 2 \times \left[\left(\frac{1}{1 - d \times n/360}\right)^{[1/(2 \times n)]} - 1\right]. \qquad \text{(3-11)}$$

$$BEY = r_a \times 365/360. \qquad \text{(3-12)}$$

$$r = (1 + r_a \times n/360)^{(365/n)} - 1; \qquad \text{(3-13)}$$

$$r = 2 \times [(1 + r_a \times n/360)^{[365/(2 \times n)]} - 1]. \qquad \text{(3-14)}$$

$$\text{T-bill futures } BERR = \frac{(d' \times n'/360) - (d \times n/360)}{1 - (d' \times n'/360)} \times \frac{360}{n' - n}$$

$$\text{(3-15)}$$

$$BPV = 24.66 \times (1 - .25 \times d)^{5.056} \qquad \text{(3-16)}$$

$$BPV = 24.66 \times (1 - .25 \times d)^{3.028} \qquad \text{(3-17)}$$

$$BPV = 24.66/(1 + .25 \times r_a)^{3.06} \qquad \text{(3-18)}$$
annually compounded, or

$$BPV = 24.66/(1 + .125 \times r_a)^{1.03} \qquad \text{(3-19)}$$
semiannually compounded
where
$r_a = (100 - \text{futures price})/100.$

$$f = \frac{C}{8} - \left(\frac{C}{8} - 1\right) \times \frac{1}{1.04^{\text{Int}(2 \times M)}} \qquad \text{(3-20a)}$$

$$CF = \frac{f + C/200}{1.04^{.5}} - \frac{C}{400} \qquad \text{(3-20b)}$$

$$BERR = \frac{P_F \times CF + AI' - (P_C + AI)}{P_C + AI} \times \frac{360}{n} \qquad \text{(3-21)}$$

$$\text{Avg. } CF = \text{Avg. price/BBI} \times \text{coefficient} \qquad \text{(3-22a)}$$

$$\text{Fwd. Avg. Price} = \text{Avg. Price} \times (1 + (r - y) \times 360/n) \qquad \text{(3-22b)}$$

Variable Names Used in Chapter 6

BPV	*Basis Point Value*
C	Call Price
P	Put Price

r	Continuously compounded *rate*
Y	Current *Y*ield on a coupon security, expressed on a continuously compounded basis.
t	*T*ime to expiration
U	*U*nderlying price: U_n = *n*ow, U_x = at e*x*piration; U_h = *h*ighest price, U_l = *l*owest price
h	short-term rate minus current yield
S	*S*trike
e	Natural log base, 2.718281828
$N(x)$	Standard *N*atural distribution function
$N'(x)$	*N* prime; the derivative of $N_{(x)}$
mdr	*M*ean *D*aily *R*eturn
π	*P*i, a constant, 3.141592654
p	*P*robability of an event occurring

$$BPV_{option} = BPV_{underlying} \times Delta_{option}. \qquad (6\text{-}1)$$

Call Premium $\qquad\qquad\qquad\qquad\qquad\qquad\qquad\qquad (6\text{-}2)$

$$C = e^{-r \times t}[U \times e^{(h \times t)} \times N(d_1) - S \times N(d_2)]$$

Put Premium $\qquad\qquad\qquad\qquad\qquad\qquad\qquad\qquad (6\text{-}3)$

$$P = e^{-r \times t}[U \times e^{(h \times t)} \times (N(d_1) - 1) - S \times (N(d_2) - 1)]$$

In the above,

$$d_1 = [\ln (U \times e^{(h \times t)}/S) + .5 \times V^2 \times t]/(v \times t^{.5})$$
$$d_2 = d_1 - V \times t^{.5}$$

Call Delta $\qquad\qquad\qquad\qquad\qquad\qquad\qquad\qquad\qquad (6\text{-}4)$

$$Delta_c = e^{(h-r) \times t} \times N(d_1)$$

Put Delta $\qquad\qquad\qquad\qquad\qquad\qquad\qquad\qquad\qquad (6\text{-}5)$

$$Delta_P = e^{(h-r) \times t} \times (N(d_1) - 1)$$

Put, Call Gamma $\qquad\qquad\qquad\qquad\qquad\qquad\qquad\qquad (6\text{-}6)$

$$Gamma = \frac{N'(d_1)}{U \times V \times t^{.5}}$$

Put Theta $\qquad\qquad\qquad\qquad\qquad\qquad\qquad\qquad\qquad (6\text{-}7)$

$$Theta_p = e^{-rt} \times \left\{ \frac{U}{2 \times t^{.5}} \times N(d_1) + S \times e^{ht} \times (h - r) \right.$$

$$\left. \times [N(d_1) - 1] + S \times r \times [N(d_2) - 1] \right\}$$

Call Theta (6-8)

$$Theta_c = e^{-rt} \times \left[\frac{U}{2 \times t^{.5}} \times N(d_1) + S \times e^{ht} \times (h - r) \times N(d_1) \right.$$

$$\left. + S \times r \times N(d_2) \right]$$

$$\text{mdr} = \sum_{t=2}^{n} \ln (U_t/U_{t-1})/(n - 1). \tag{6-9a}$$

$$V = \sqrt{\frac{\sum\limits_{t=2}^{n} [\ln (U_t/U_{t-1}) - \text{mdr}]^2}{n - 2}} \times \text{obs. per year.} \tag{6-9b}$$

$$N(x) = 1 - 1/\sqrt{2\pi} \times e^{-(x^2/2)} \times (b_1 \times k + b_2 \times k^2 + b_3 \times k^3$$

$$+ b_4 \times k^4 + b_5 \times k^5) \tag{6-10a}$$

$$N(-x) = 1 - N(x). \tag{6-10b}$$

$$P \geqslant 0 \tag{6-11}$$

$$C \geqslant 0 \tag{6-12}$$

$$P = Se^{-rt} - U_n + C \tag{6-13}$$

$$C = U_n - Se^{-rt} + P. \tag{6-14}$$

$$C > U_n - Se^{-rt} \tag{6-15}$$

$$P > Se^{-rt} - U_n. \tag{6-16}$$

$$C_1 = e^{-rt} \times \sum_{U_x=S}^{\infty} p_{U_x} \times (U_x - S). \tag{6-17a}$$

$$C_2 = U_n - Se^{-rt} + \sum_{U_x=0}^{S} p_{U_x}(S - U_x) \times e^{-rt} \tag{6-17b}$$

$$P_1 = e^{-rt} \times \sum_{U_x=0}^{S} p_{U_x} \times (S - U_x). \tag{6-18a}$$

$$P_2 = Se^{-rt} - U_n + \sum_{U_x=S}^{\infty} p_{U_x} \times (U_x - S) \times e^{-rt}. \qquad (6\text{-}18b)$$

$$C = \max [C_1, C_2], \qquad (6\text{-}17c)$$

$$P = \max [P_1, P_2]. \qquad (6\text{-}18c)$$

$$X = \frac{U_n - U_1}{C_h - C_1} \qquad (6\text{-}19a)$$

$$B = (U_h - X \times C_h) \times e^{-rt} \qquad (6\text{-}19b)$$

$$C = \frac{U_n - B}{X} \qquad (6\text{-}19c)$$

Further Examples and Discussion

Chapter 1

Examples

The following is a portfolio of assets and the liabilities which fund them:

A: Government pure-discount bill, face value $1,000,000, matures in exactly one year, market value $909,091.

A: Government bond, face value $100,000, next cash settlement date tomorrow, maturing in exactly 17 years, coupon 12% per year paid semiannually, next coupon due exactly 6 months from today.

L: Insurance company loan, book value $471,312, interest and principal due according to the following schedule:

$250,000 due in 6 months
$125,000 due in 9 months
$125,000 due in 1 year.

L: Bank-floating rate, 5-year revolving credit; present borrowings plus accrued interest, $556,905.

Important: Assume that the rate of return required by the market is the same for all maturities and all assets and liabilities on the balance sheet.

1. Calculate the BPV of this balance sheet. Ignore compounding assumptions.

2. Rates rise uniformly by 0.1%. Estimate by what dollar amount the value of the balance sheet will change.

3. The yield curve twists, changing shape from the solid line to the dotted line on the diagram below. Do not do detailed calculations, but explain:

   a. How will the value of the balance sheet change and why?

   b. Would the BPV you calculated above accurately predict the change in value caused by the twist in the curve?

   Explain.

   c. How will the duration and BPV of the balance sheet change as a result of the twist in the yield curve?

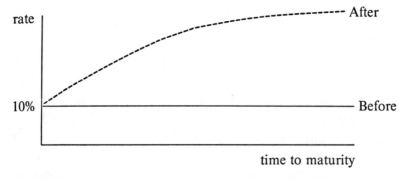

4. Quantify the effect on the first liability in the above balance sheet of a twist in the yield curve if before the twist the curve was defined as $r = .10 + (0 \times b)$, and after the twist the yield curve is defined as $r = .1005 + (.0003 \times b)$.

5. On 6/15/85 the 11 3/4 T-bond maturing on 11/15/2014 sells for 99½% of par (face) value. What is the bond's basis point value? What is its duration?

6. The bond in Example 5 is callable at par on 11/15/2009. In other words, the government has the right to buy the bond back on that date at a price of $100 per $100 face value. Are you completely comfortable assuming a 2014 maturity date in light of this? Conversely, are you completely comfortable assuming a maturity date of 11/15/2009 for the purpose of calculating BPV? How large a difference is there between these two assumptions in terms of BPV? Is there a third alternative? Is there a fourth alternative?

Discussion

1. To calculate the balance sheet's BPV, calculate the BPV of
    each asset and liability. Add up the asset BPVs and subtract
    off the liability BPVs. The resulting net BPV measures by
    how much the value of equity will increase if rates decline by
    one basis point (or by how much equity value will fall if rates
    rise by one basis point).

    First asset:

    You have a market price; use it to obtain a market rate.

    $$r = \left(\frac{1,000,000}{909,091}\right)^{(1/1)} - 1 = .10$$

    $$BPV = 909,091 \times .0001/1.10 \times 1 = 82.64$$

    Second Asset:

    The market rate is the same for all assets and liabilities,
    10%.

Price of bond at yield of 9.995%:	116,238.41
Price of bond at yield of 10.005%:	−116,147.42
BPV is the difference in the above prices:	90.99

    First Liability:

    This liability is difficult to analyze because of the un-
    even cash flow amounts and the unequal intervals at
    which the cash flows are due. The simplest strategy is to
    calculate the BPV of each cash flow separately, then
    sum.

    $$\frac{250,000}{1.09995^5} - \frac{250,000}{1.10005^5} = 10.83$$

    $$\frac{125,000}{1.09995^{.75}} - \frac{125,000}{1.10005^{.75}} = 7.93$$

    $$\frac{125,000}{1.09995^1} - \frac{125,000}{1.10005^1} = \frac{10.33}{29.09} = BPV$$

    You can calculate the present values of the cash flows,
    then use the duration approach to *BPV*:

$$\frac{250{,}000}{1.10^5} \times \frac{.0001}{1.10} \times .5 = 10.83$$

$$\frac{125{,}000}{1.10^{.75}} \times \frac{.0001}{1.10} \times .75 = 7.93$$

$$\frac{125{,}000}{1.10^1} \times \frac{.0001}{1.10} \times 1 = \frac{10.33}{29.09}$$

As a third alternative, you could calculate the duration of the liability as a whole, and then use the duration to BPV formula on the result.

$$D = \frac{\left(\frac{250{,}000}{1.10^5}\right) \times .5 + \left(\frac{125{,}000}{1.10^{.75}}\right) \times .75 + \left(\frac{125{,}000}{1.10^1}\right) \times 1}{\frac{250{,}000}{1.10^5} + \frac{125{,}000}{1.10^{.75}} + \frac{125{,}000}{1.10^1}} = .683425$$

$$BPV = \left(\frac{250{,}000}{1.10^5} + \frac{125{,}000}{1.10^{.75}} + \frac{125{,}000}{1.10^1}\right) \times \frac{.0001}{1.10} \times .683425$$

$$= 29.09$$

Second Liability: Floating rate liabilities have a BPV of 0.

Balance Sheet BPV:

$$\begin{array}{r} 82.64 \\ + \ 90.00 \\ - \ 29.09 \\ 0 \\ \hline 144.54 \end{array}$$

2. A .10% rise in rates is a ten basis point rise. The balance sheet will decline in value by

$$10 \times 144.54 + \$1{,}445.40$$

This result might be inaccurate for two reasons: first, BPV is perfectly accurate only for very small changes in rates; second, you ignored differences in compounding assumptions in calculating the BPV of the second asset.

3. a) Rates rose overall and the balance sheet has a positive BPV. Therefore, its value will decline.

b) The BPV you measured in the first problem would be difficult to use to predict the size of the decline in value accurately. First, rates changed by a different amount for each time to maturity; what size of rate change would you choose? Second, most of the asset cash flows are affected by much larger rate shifts than most of the liability cash flows. It is, therefore, likely that, whatever value you choose for the change in rates, you overstated the rate change for the liabilities and understated the rate change for the assets.

c) The assets declined in value and duration much more than the liabilities; the BPV of the balance sheet would shrink as a result of the rate shift.

4. The value of the first liability before the rate shift is

$$\frac{250,000}{1.10^{.5}} + \frac{125,000}{1.10^{.75}} + \frac{125,000}{1.10^{1}} = \$468,378.55$$

The rate at which the cash flows are discounted is 10% in every case. After the rate shift, a different rate is used to determine the present value of each cash flow.

Time of receipt of cash flow	Rate
6 months	$.1005 + .0003 \times .5 = .10065$
9 months	$.1005 + .0003 \times .75 = .100725$
1 year	$.1005 + .0003 \times 1 = .1008$

The present value of the cash flows has changed to

$$\frac{250,000}{1.10065^{.5}} + \frac{125,000}{1.100725^{.75}} + \frac{125,000}{1.1008^{1}} = 468,168.09;$$

a decline in value of $210.46.

5. The yield to maturity of the bond is 11.808%.
    The price at a yield of 11.803 is $99,542.91.
    The price at a yield of 11.813 is   99,461.45.
    The BPV (per $100,000 face value) is $ 81.46.

    The duration is $81.46/99,500 \times 1.11808/.0001 = 9.15$ years.

6. The bond is selling at close to the call price of 100. While it is slightly more likely that the bond will *not* be called, it is difficult to predict the level of rates which will prevail more than 20 years hence. You cannot be completely comfortable assuming that the bond's life will end in 2009 or 2014. The BPV calculated assuming that the bond is called is 79.22 per $100,000 face value, versus $81.46 assuming no call. A third alternative is to use a date midway between 11/15/2014 and 11/15/2009. A fourth alternative is to use an option pricing formula to calculate the interest sensitivity of the call feature.

Chapter 2

Examples

1. You are an investor wishing to maximize your return over nine months. You are considering these pure discount government securities:

Security	Yield	Price
Three-month bill*	10%	$976,454
Six-month bill	12	944,911
Nine-month bill	14	906,403

*Hypothetical; not discount priced

Futures contracts are available which call for delivery of a three-month, $1,000,000 face value bill, three months or six months hence. The futures are priced as follows:

Delivery Date	Yield on Deliverable	Price
Three months hence	13%	$969,908
Six months hence	19	957,444

How many different ways could you create a security with a single cash flow after nine months (ignore margin)? What would be the return on each? The duration? Which is most profitable?

Term repo rates are as follows:

Term	Rate
Three months	10.5%
Six months	12.5
Nine months	14.5

Reverse repo rates are ½% lower than corresponding term repo rates at these rates. Is arbitrage profitable, given the above prices?

2. Challenge Question. Answer each part before proceeding to the next. Assume a flat yield curve.

a. The basis point value of a futures contract has been defined as the basis point value of the security which will be delivered, as it will appear on the delivery date. Consider a hypothetical futures contract on a $1,000,000 90-day bill. The deliverable bill today has six months to maturity and sells for $950,000. The futures price translates to an invoice price at delivery of $975,000. What is the BPV of the futures contract?

b. A balance sheet is defined as an asset (cash inflow receivable) and a liability (cash outflow due) which supports the asset. The BPV of a balance sheet is the sum of the BPVs of the assets less the sum of the BPVs of the liabilities. Describe the bill futures contract in (a) as a balance sheet.

c. Using the methodology used to measure a balance sheet's BPV, measure the BPV of the futures contract described in (a). Assume a flat yield curve with a level equal to the rate implied by the futures price.

d. Why is the BPV you just calculated different from the one calculated for part (a)? Devise a mathematical formula which accurately measures the difference between the BPVs.

e. Why is the BPV calculated in part (a) the more appropriate measure of interest sensitivity?

f. Why doesn't arbitrage activity adjust for the timing of variation margin cash flows?

3. a. The June 1986 Treasury bill futures are priced at 92.80, which corresponds to an invoice price of $982,000 for

delivery of a $1,000,000 face value, 90 day bill. What is the BPV of the futures contract?

b. Use arbitrage arguments to prove your answer in part (a), assuming that the yield curve is flat.

c. Challenge Question. Use arbitrage arguments to verify your answer to part (a), if the yield curve is described by the formula

$$r_T = .0722 + .0056 \times T$$

where
  T = the time to maturity in years

Assume that the June contract is three months away from delivery.

Discussion

1. There are three nine-month investments possible:
    1) Buy and hold the nine-month cash bill.
    2) Buy the six-month cash bills and at the same time buy the futures which will result in delivery of a three-month cash bill in six months. Buy enough futures so that the maturity value of the cash bills will be exactly the amount required to take delivery on the futures. In six months, take delivery on the futures and hold the delivered bills until maturity.
    3) Buy the three-month cash bills; buy the futures which result in delivery in three months; buy the futures which result in delivery in six months. Buy enough of the first futures so that the maturity value of the cash bills will be just sufficient to pay for delivery under the first set of futures. Buy enough of the second set of futures so that the maturity value of the bills delivered into the first set of futures will be just sufficient to pay for delivery on the second set of futures.

Returns:
1) The nine-month cash bill earns 14%.
2) $[1.12^5 \times 1.19^{25}]^{(1/.75)} = .1429$ or 14.29%
3) $[1.10^{25} \times 1.13^{25} \times 1.19^{25}]^{(1/.75)} - 1 = .1394$ or 13.94%

Duration: In each case, the duration is nine months.

Most profitable: The second alternative.

Arbitrage:

1) Buy (sell) six-month bill; sell (buy) futures for delivery in three months.

$$BERR = (969,908 - 944,911)/944,911 \times 360/90 = .1058$$

The three-month term repo is 10.5 percent. A cash and carry is profitable; a reverse cash and carry is, therefore, unprofitable.

2) Buy (sell) the nine-month cash bill; sell (buy) the futures for delivery in six months.

$$BERR = (957,444 - 906,403)/906,403 \times 360/180 = .1126$$

The six-month term repo is 12.50. A cash and carry is quite unprofitable. This suggests that a reverse cash and carry might be profitable. The six-month term reverse repo rate is 12 percent. The reverse cash and carry profit is, therefore, the equivalent of earning 74 basis points on $906,403 for 180 days.

2. (a) Forward rate $= 1,000,000^{(1/.25)}/975,000 - 1 = .1066$

Futures $BPV = 975,000 \times .0001/1.1066 \times .25 = 22.02.$

(b) The futures contract consists of an asset—$1 million receivable on the maturity date of the deliverable bill and a liability—$975,000 payable on the futures delivery date.

(c) Time to deliverable bill maturity: .5 years.

BPV of maturity value:

$$(1,000,000/1.1066^{.5}) \times (.0001/1.1066) \times .5 = 42.95.$$

The delivery date is in .25 years.

BPV of invoice price:

$$(975,000/1.066^{.25}) \times (.0001/1.1066) \times .25 = 21.47.$$

The balance sheet $BPV = 42.95 - 21.47 = 21.48.$

(d) The futures BPV is the change in present value of the deliverable security as of the delivery date. The measurement done in part (b) present-values the futures cash flows back to today. The relationship between the two is

$$21.48 \times 1.1066^{.25} = 22.02$$

(e) Futures margin flows pay today for changes in an invoice price which will not be paid until the delivery date. In most applications, predicting futures margin flows is the ultimate objective of our analysis. Thus, the method used in (a) is the most appropriate.

(f) Arbitragers cannot predict the direction of interest rate changes and so cannot know if they will profit or lose from investing margin inflows or financing margin outflows.

3. (a) Rate $= (1,000,000/982,000)^{(365/90)} - 1 = .076446$

   $BPV = 982,000 \times (.0001/1.0764) \times (90/365) = 22.49$

(b) Futures price = cash price + cost of financing until delivery.

   Suppose the futures is 92 days away from delivery. If the market rate were .07635, the cash bill would be priced today at

   $$1,000,000/1.07635^{(182/365)} = 963,977.76$$

   The fair futures price would be

   Deliverable cash price $\times (1 + \text{financing rate})^{(\text{days to delivery}/365)}$

   $$963,977.76 \times 1.07635^{(92/365)} = \$982,021.62$$

   If the market rate were .07645, the fair futures price would be

   $$(1,000,000/1.07645^{(182/365)}) \times (1.07645)^{(92/365)} = 981,999.13$$

   a change in fair futures price of 22.49.

(c) Term repo $= .0736$.

   $YTM = .075$.

$$1,000,000/1.075^{.5} = 964,495.64$$

If the term repo and *YTM* were ½ basis point lower,

$$\text{Cash price} = 1,000,000/1.07495^{.5} = 964,508.08$$

The Futures price would be

$$964,508.08 \times 1.07355^{.25} = 981,773.80.$$

Were rates half a basis point higher,

$$\text{Cash price} = 1,000,000/1.070505^{.5} = 964,463.21$$

and the futures price would be

$$964,463.31 \times 1.07365.25 = 981,751.09$$

a difference of 22.70, close but not identical to the results obtained in (b). The difference must be attributed to violation of the flat curve assumption implicit in *BPV* analysis.

Chapter 3

Examples

1. Derive and explain intuitively Equation 3-5.
2. Intuitively, why does the discount move less than 1 percent for a 1 percent move in the annually compounded rate?
3. Derive and explain intuitively Equation 3-8.
4. Why can't you use Equation 3-9 to compare a one year T-bill to a one-year coupon T-note?
5. Derive and explain intuitively Equations 3-10 through 3-14.
6. Derive and explain intuitively Equations 3-15 and 3-16.
7. You intend to deliver a 10⅝ bond maturing on August 15, 2015 (not callable) into the March 1987 bond futures contract, currently priced at 90-20. How many contracts do you sell? What effective selling prices do you hope to obtain in March 1987?

Discussion

1. $M = I \times (1 + r_a \times n/360)$

$$I' = M/1 + r_a'n'/360$$

Therefore,

$$I' = \frac{I \times (1 + r_a n/360)}{1 + r_a'n'/360}$$

$$= I \times \frac{360 + r_a n}{360 + r_a'n'}$$

2. The discount expresses return as a fraction of face value. A rate expresses return as a fraction of initial investment. Because face value does not change but initial investment declines when rates rise, the discount changes more slowly than the rate.

3. Price given discount equals $F \times (1 - d \times n/360)$. Consider a T-bill with a maturity value of $1. Then the straight-line, 360-day rate of return is

$$r_a = (M/I) - 1 \times (360/n) = [1/(1 - d \times n/360)] - 1 \times 360/n.$$

4 The yield on the T-Note by custom is calculated assuming semi-annual compounding. The bond equivalent yield is a straight-line rate.

5. Equation 3-10:

$$r = \left(\frac{F}{P}\right)^{(365/n)} - 1.$$

If $F = 1$, $P = 1 - d \times n/360$.

Therefore, to get r from d,

$$r = \left(\frac{1}{1 - d \times n/360}\right)^{(365/n)} - 1.$$

Equation 3-11:

$$r_2 = 2 \times \left(\frac{F}{P}\right)^{[1/(2 \times n)]} - 1.$$

If $F = 1$, $P = 1 - d \times n/360$.

Therefore,

$$r_2 = 2 \times \left(\frac{1}{1 - d \times n/360}\right)^{[1/(2n)]} - 1.$$

Equation 3-12:

This equation already describes a straight-line rate. To convert it to a 365-day-year basis, by multiplying the add-on rate by 365/360.

Equation 3-13:

$$r_a = \left(\frac{F}{P} - 1\right) \times \frac{360}{n}$$

$$r = \left(\frac{F}{P}\right)^{(365/n)} - 1$$

$$1 + r_a \times \frac{n}{360} = \frac{F}{P}$$

Therefore,

$$r = (1 + r_a \times n/360)^{(360/n)} - 1.$$

Equation 3-14:

From Appendix 1,

$$r_2 = 2 \times \left(\frac{F}{P}\right)^{[365/(2\times n)]} - 1$$

as shown above, $F/P = (1 + r_a \times n/360)$
Therefore,

$$r_2 = 2 \times [(1 + r_a \times n/360)^{[365/(2\times n)]} - 1].$$

6. Equation 3-15:

$$BERR = \frac{\text{Futures Invoice Price} - \text{Cash Price}}{\text{Cash Price}} \times \frac{360}{n}$$

Suppose the futures were on a $1 face value bill. Then

$$\text{Futures Invoice Price} = 1 - d \times n/360$$
$$\text{Deliverable Cash Price} = 1 - d' \times n'/360$$

$$BERR = \frac{1 - d \times n/360 - (1 - d' \times n'/360)}{1 - d' \times n'/360} \times \frac{360}{n' - n}$$

Rearranging the numerator to cancel terms,

$$BERR = \frac{(d' \times n'/360) - (d \times n/360)}{1 - (d' \times n'/360)} \times \frac{360}{n' - n}$$

Equation 3-16

From Equation 1-5, $BPV = P \times .0001/(1 + r) \times D$

From Equation 3-7, $P = F \times (1 - d \times n/360)$

From Equation 3-10, $r = \left(\dfrac{1}{1 - d \times n/360}\right)^{(365/n)} - 1.$

Set $n = 90$, and $F = 1,000,000$.

$$BPV = 1,000,000 \times (1 - d \times 90/360) \times \frac{.0001}{\left(\dfrac{1}{1 - d \times 90/360}\right)^{(365/90)}}$$

$$\times \frac{90}{365}$$

$$BPV = 1,000,000 \times .0001 \times 90/365 \times \frac{1 - d \times 90/360}{\left(\dfrac{1}{1 - d \times 90/360}\right)^{(365/90)}}$$

$$BPV = 24.66 \times (1 - .25d)^{5.056}$$

7. You sell *CF* futures for each $100,000 face value of the bonds you intend to deliver, where *CF* is the official conversion factor for delivering the 10% bonds into the March bond futures contract. The conversion factor for the 10% bonds is 1.2921.

The price you hope to obtain is

99-20/32 × 1.2921 = 128.7255 percent of par, plus coupon accrual.

Coupon accrual will vary depending on which day in March you elect to deliver the bonds.

Chapter 4

Examples

1. a) It is June 19, 1986. A Treasury bill maturing December 26, 1986 is priced at 6.15. What would you pay for $1 million face value of these bills?

    b) Completely hedge $100 million of the above bills in the September 1986 Treasury bill futures contract priced at 94-16. Assume 90 days from delivery to maturity of the deliverable bill.

    c) The Treasury bills maturing September 25, 1986 are priced at 6.05. The December 26, 1986 bills are deliverable into the September bill futures contract. Together with the prices supplied in part (a), what does this imply about the cash-futures basis in the September bills? How does this affect the expected performance of your hedge?

2. a) It is June 19, 1986. Buy and completely hedge $5 million of the 8⅞% notes maturing February 15, 1986, priced at 107-16, using the September 1986 bond futures priced at 95-19. Assume delivery on September 21, 1986. The 14% bonds of November 15, 2011, callable in 2006, are cheapest-to-deliver.

    b) Do you think the 14% bonds in a) will be called? How will this affect your hedge calculations?

    c) Hedge the above 8⅞% notes using September 1986 T-note futures contracts, priced at 99-06. The 8⅞% notes are cheapest-to-deliver. Assume delivery on September 21, 1986.

    d) Why isn't the hedge ratio in (c) simply equal to the conversion factor for the 8⅞% notes?

    e) Hedge the 8⅞% notes in the September 1986 note futures to protect their market value as of 94 days from today (June 19th). What arbitrage strategy does this hedge resemble?

    f) How would you adjust your hedge in part (e) to compensate for the timing of margin flows? Assume you can borrow and lend margin funds at 6½% (annually compounded). How would this adjustment change between now and September? How significantly do you think this adjustment will affect your hedge performance?

Discussion

1. (a) There are 190 days between June 19 and December 26. Treasury bills are customarily sold for next business day settlement. A bill bought on June 19 for settlement on the 20th would sell for

$$1{,}000{,}000 \times (1 - .0615 \times 189/360) = 967{,}712.50.$$

(b) The annually compounded rate of return on the bill is

$$\left(\frac{1}{1 - .0615 \times 189/360}\right)^{(365/189)} - 1 = .0654.$$

Their BPV per million face value is

$$967{,}712.50 \times .0001/1.0654 \times 189/365 = 47.03$$

The BPV of a futures contract is

$$24.66 \times 1 - .25 \times [(100 - 94.5)/100]^{5.056} = 22.99$$

To hedge the bills, you would sell

$$110 \times (47.03/22.99) = 204.56 \text{ or } 205 \text{ December bill futures.}$$

The breakeven repo rate of the December bill futures is

$$\frac{.0605 \times 189/360 - .0550 \times 90/360}{1 - (.00605 \times 189/360)} \times \frac{360}{189 - 90} = .0678$$

The September bills yield a straight-line, 360-day rate equivalent of

$$1/(1 - d \times 99/360) \times 1 \times 360/99 = .0615.$$

The BERR is 63 basis points higher than the Treasury rate of comparable term, suggesting that the futures may be expensive relative to the deliverable bill. Since you will be selling the futures to hedge, this expensive-ness of the futures may improve your experienced return on the hedged position.

2. (a) The BPV of the 8⅞ notes is 703.37 per million dollars face value.

   The BPV of the bond futures is 143.88 per contract.

   The conversion factor of the cheapest-to-deliver 14% is 1.5938.

   To hedge, sell

   $$5 \times (703.37/143.88) \times 1.5938 = 38.95 \text{ or } 39 \text{ September bond futures.}$$

   (b) The 14% bonds are likely to be called. Recalculating BPV to call rather than to maturity gives a BPV of 133.91. The hedge ratio becomes

   $$5 \times (703.37/133.91) \times 1.5938 = 41.86 \text{ or } 42 \text{ September bond futures.}$$

   (c) The BPV of the note futures is 66.85 per contract, with a conversion factor of 1.0562.

   To hedge, sell

   $$5 \times (703.37/66.85) \times 1.0562 = 55.56 \text{ or } 56 \text{ note futures.}$$

   (d) We are hedging the notes' value as of today, not as of the delivery date, as in a cash and carry. Therefore, we need to sell more than CF futures per $100,000 of the notes.

   (e) Sell

   $$5 \times 10 \times 1.0562 = 52.8 \text{ or } 53 \text{ note futures.}$$

   This hedge resembles a cash and carry arbitrage.

   (f) Reduce the hedge position so that margin flows equal the present value of the change in invoice price. Sell

   $$\frac{52.8}{1.065^{(94/365)}} = 52 \text{ contracts}$$

   As time passes, the days left to the hedge termination date will decline. In perhaps 30 days the hedge should be increased to 53 contracts to reflect the shorter time left to the end of the hedge. The adjustment will only make a 2% difference in hedge performance.

Chapter 5

Examples

1. Refer to the example discussed on page 97. The fixed-rate payor enters into the swap agreement and immediately thereafter experiences a business reversal which reduces the payor's perceived creditworthiness in the marketplace. The payor anticipates that when he or she issues new three-month CDs in three months and each time thereafter, he or she will pay 120 basis points over LIBOR on his short-term liabilities.

   What is the impact on the payor's experienced cost of funds as measured by IRR? Spread to Treasury?

2. What is the new BPV and SPV of his liability position?

Discussion

1. The cash flows associated with the swap will change after three months. The cost of servicing short-term debt will then exceed the floating rate payment stream by 30,000 per quarter rather 10,000. We can evaluate this new stream of cash flows using the techniques described in Chapter 5. Set up a spread sheet with the following columns:

	A	*B*
1	Time	Swap C.F.
2	0	10,000,000
3	3	− 10,000
4	6	− 414,500
5	9	− 30,000
6	12	− 414,500
7	15	− 30,000
8	18	− 414,500
9	21	− 30,000
10	24	−10,414,500
11		
12	IRR	= 4 ∗ @ IRR (.10,B2 . . . B10)
13	Semi IRR = 2*[(1 + B12/4)^2-1]

On calculation, the IRR value in cell B12 will equal .0870 or
8.70%, and the semiannual equivalent in B13 will equal .0879
or 8.79%.

	A	B
1	Time	Swap C.F.
2	0	10,000,000
3	3	− 10,000
4	6	− 414,500
5	9	− 30,000
6	12	− 414,500
7	15	− 30,000
8	18	− 414,500
9	21	− 30,000
10	24	−10,414,500
11		
12	IRR = 0.086995844	
13	SEMI IRR = 0.087941878	

To determine the spread to Treasury, add two new columns
to the spreadsheet.

	A	B	C	D	E
1	Time	Swap C.F.	Treas. Yld	Markup	PValue
2	0	10,000,000	.00		+B2/(1+(C2+D2)/2)^(A2/G)
3	3	− 10,000	.0574	+ D2	+ E2
4	6	− 414,500	.063	+ D3	+ E3
5	9	− 30,000	.064	+ D4	+ E4
6	12	− 414,500	.065	+ D5	+ E5
7	15	− 30,000	.0669	+ D6	+ E6
8	18	− 414,500	.0685	+ D7	+ E7
9	21	− 30,000	.0699	+ D8	+ E8
10	24	−10,414,500	.074	+ D9	+ E9
11					
12					NPV = @SUM(E2 ... E10)
13					

Guess a spread over Treasury yields which will cause the
present value of the cash outflows in column E to sum to the
notional amount of the swap. Plug the value into D2; change
your guess until the NPV in column E12 equals (approximately) zero. At this point, the markup in D2 will equal the
spread to Treasury, .017148 or 1.71%.

	A	B	C	D	E
1	Time	Swap C.F.	Treas. Yld	Markup	PValue
2	0	10,000,000	.00	.017148	10,000,000
3	3	− 10,000	.0574	.017148	− 9,818.68
4	6	− 414,500	.063	.017148	− 398,529.00
5	9	− 30,000	.064	.017148	− 28,262.50
6	12	− 414,500	.065	.017148	− 382,438.00
7	15	− 30,000	.0669	.017148	− 27,066.10
8	18	− 414,500	.0685	.017148	− 365,503.00
9	21	− 30,000	.0699	.017148	− 25,844.10
10	24	−10,414,500	.0711	.017148	−8,762,541.00
11					
12	IRR = 0.086995844				NPV = −4.62181
13	SEMI IRR = 0.087941878				

2. To calculate the basis point value, add .0001 to the value in D2 from the work done in a). The number in E12 will equal the basis point value, $1791.94.

	A	B	C	D	E
1	Time	Swap C.F.	Treas. Yld	Markup	PValue
2	0	10,000,000	.00	.017248	10,000,000
3	3	− 10,000	.0574	.017248	− 9,818.44
4	6	− 414,500	.063	.017248	− 398,510.00
5	9	− 30,000	.064	.017248	− 28,260.50
6	12	− 414,500	.065	.017248	− 382,401.00
7	15	− 30,000	.0669	.017248	− 27,062.90
8	18	− 414,500	.0685	.017248	− 365,450.00
9	21	− 30,000	.0699	.017248	− 25,839.80
10	24	−10,414,500	.0711	.017248	−8,760,863.00
11					
12	IRR = 0.086995844				NPV = 1791.938
13	SEMI IRR = 0.087941878				

To calculate the SPV, plug the original spread to Treasury back into D2. Modify cells D3 to D10 as follows:

3	.000025 + D2
4	.000025 + D3
5	.000025 + D4
6	.000025 + D5
7	.000025 + D6
8	.000025 + D7

$$9 \qquad .000025 + D8$$
$$10 \qquad .000025 + D9$$

The number in E12 equals the slope point value, $3489.80.

	A	B	C	D	E
1	Time	Swap C.F.	Treas. Yld	Markup	PValue
2	0	10,000,000	.00	.017148	10,000,000
3	3	− 10,000	.0574	.017173	− 9,818.62
4	6	− 414,500	.063	.017198	− 398,519.00
5	9	− 30,000	.064	.017223	− 28,261.00
6	12	− 414,500	.065	.017248	− 382,401.00
7	15	− 30,000	.0669	.017273	− 27,062.10
8	18	− 414,500	.0685	.017298	− 365,424.00
9	21	− 30,000	.0699	.017323	− 25,836.50
10	24	−10,414,500	.074	.017348	−8,759,185.00
11					
12	IRR = 0.086995844				NPV = 3489.861
13	SEMI IRR = 0.087941878				

Chapter 6

Examples

1. A 10% Treasury bond is currently priced at 110% of par. The short-term financing rate for Treasury securities is 7%. Over the last three weeks, the bond has traded at the following prices. There are 260 trading days in a year.

Day	
1	105-00
2	105-08
3	105-04
4	105-10
5	105-16
6	108-00
7	107-28
8	109-00
9	109-08
10	109-31
11	110-16
12	110-09
13	110-12
14	110-03
15	110-00 (today)

You are able to buy a put or call on this cash bond with half a year to expiration and a strike price of 107% of par. What premium would you be willing to pay for each?

2. A put has a delta of .4 and a gamma of .06.
   a. The underlying security falls in price by 1/32. By how much does the put premium change?
   b. The underlying price declines by 3 points. By how much does the put premium change?

Discussion

1. You have most of the variables required to use the Black-Scholes formula:

$$
\begin{aligned}
U &= 110 & r &= .07 \\
S &= 107 & y &= .10 \\
t &= .5 & h &= r - y = -.03
\end{aligned}
$$

You need an estimate of market volatility, v. Your only source for this input is the price history, which might be too short to produce comfortable results. Nonetheless, calculate the historical volatility as follows:

- calculate the continuously compounded daily returns for days 2 through 15, $\ln (U_t/U_{t-1}) = R$.
- calculate the average daily return

$$
\sum_{t=2}^{15} \ln (U_t/U_{t-1})/14 = \bar{R}
$$

- calculate for each day, the squared difference between the daily return and the average daily return,

$$
(R_t - \bar{R})^2
$$

- the historical annualized volatility will equal

$$
\sqrt{\frac{\sum\limits_{t=2}^{15} (R_t - \bar{R})^2}{(14 - 1)}} \times 260
$$

As calculated in a spread sheet, the above procedure appears as follows:

Day	Price	Rate	$(R-AVR)\hat{}2$
1	105		
2	105.25	0.002378122	0.000011041
3	105.125	−0.00118835	0.000000892
4	105.3125	0.001782002	0.000020351
5	105.5	0.001778832	0.000002374
6	108	0.023420274	0.000002384
7	107.875	−0.00115807	0.000403906 Vol=0.108929
8	109	0.010374732	0.000020078 (approximately all)
·9	109.25	0.002290951	0.000049728
10	109.9687	0.006557400	0.000001064
11	110.5	0.004819286	0.000010462
12	110.2812	−0.00198160	0.000002239
13	110.375	0.000849738	0.000028137
14	110.0937	−0.00255138	0.000006116
15	110	−0.00085190	0.000034506

Avg. Ret. = 0.003322858
SumSqDif = 0.000593283

We estimate that $V = .11$.

We can now use the Black-Scholes formula to estimate the put and call values.

$$d_1 = [\ln (110xe^{(-.03\times.5)}/107) + .5 \times .11^2 \times .5]/(.11 \times .5^{.5}) = .20155$$

$$d_2 = d_1 - .11 \times .5^{.5} = .12376$$

$$N(d_1) = .57987 = 1 - (1/\sqrt{2\pi}) \times e^{-(d1/2)} \times .319381530 \times k$$
$$- .356563782 \times k^2 + 1.781477937 \times k^3$$
$$- 1.821255978 \times k^4 + 1.330274429 \times k^5$$

where $k = 1/(1 + .2316419 \times d_1) = .955395065$

$$N(d_2) = .54926 = 1 - (1/\sqrt{2\pi}) \times e^{-(d2/2)} \times .319381530 \times k$$
$$- .356563782 \times k^2 + 1.781477937 \times k^3$$
$$- 1.821255978 \times k^4 + 1.330274429 \times k^5$$

where $k = 1/(1 + .2316419 \times d_2) = .972130948$

$$C = e^{(-.07\times.5)}[110 \times e^{(-.03\times.5)} \times .57987 - 107 \times .54926] = 3.93$$

$$P = e^{(-.07\times.5)}[110 \times e^{(-.03\times.5)} \times (.57987 - 1) - 107$$
$$\times (.54926 - 1)] = 2.70$$

2. a. For a small move in the underlying security price, delta indicates the change in option price. If the underlying price changes by 1/32% = .03125%, the option will change in price by .4 × .03125 = .0125 points.

   b. During larger price moves, the delta changes. Simply estimating that the put increased in price by 3 x .4 = 1.2 points would underestimate the actual price change. The gamma is an estimate of the change in delta; it suggests that the put delta will rise to .4 + 3 × .06 = .58 as the price drags. The average delta over a 3-point price move might be estimated at .4 + (3/2 × .06) = .49. The estimated change in put value would be an increase of .49 × 3 = 1.47 points.

Chapter 7

Examples

1. T-note futures are trading at 92-31 bid, 93-00 offered. You own the March 100 puts, which expire in six days. They are trading at 6-62 bid, 7-04 offered all local markets. You wish to offset your put position. You pay $30 per round-turn on commissions. Is it best to sell the put or is there another strategy which is more advantageous?

2. June Eurodollar futures are at 93.50. You own the June 92.25 Eurodollar calls, which currently trade at 1.26. The call's delta is close to 1 and its gamma, close to zero. You can invest your money at a rate of 7%. Given that you need the interest sensitivity that the call creates, is it better to hold the call to expiration or to exercise it?

Discussion

1. To sell your put with certainty, you would have to hit the bid, taking in 6.62 or $6,968.75.

   As an alternative, you could buy a futures contract at 93-00, hold the option to expiry, and deliver the futures into the put. You would take in $7000, less 30 dollars additional commission on the futures, for a net take of $6,970.00. You have offset all the put's interest sensitivity, and have created a synthetic par call with one week until expiration. The market has paid you $1.25 to do so.

2. By exercising the call, you receive a long futures position and a margin flow of 2500 × 1.25 = 3125. You can earn 3125 × .07/12 = $18.22 of interest on this margin flow between now and the option's expiration. By selling the option, you take in one basis point or $25 of time premium in addition to the $3125 intrinsic value. In a world without transaction costs, you might consider selling the call and buying a futures contract to save one basis point of time decay. Considering real world transaction costs, you are probably still better off holding the option.

Chapter 8

Examples

You wish to hedge $1 million in bonds with a basis point value totaling $1000. September bond futures trade at 93-00, and December futures at 92-00. The factored basis point value of the September bond futures is $100, and $95 for the December bond futures. You are considering a delta neutral hedge in puts on bond futures. Your alternatives are:

Month	Strike	Price	Delta	Gamma	Theta(per day)
Sep	88	0-33	.17	.05	.008
Sep	92	1-47	.41	.07	.011
Sep	96	4-01	.68	.06	.010
Dec	88	1-27	.28	.04	.007
Dec	92	3-01	.47	.05	.008
Dec	96	5-26	.65	.05	.006

In which option would you hedge if,

1. Your goal is to minimize transaction costs?
2. You fear great volatility in bond prices?
3. You wish to minimize time decay?
4. You wish to minimize total initial premium paid?

Discussion

The hedge ratio you would use in each the puts and some other pertinent data is tabled below:

Month	Strike	Hedge Qty[a]	Total Initial Prem.[b]	Total Hedge ΔBPV[c]	Ttl Daily Time Decay[d]
Sep	88	59	30,422	29.50	472
Sep	92	24	41,625	16.80	264
Sep	96	15	60,234	9.00	150
Dec	88	38	54,031	13.72	266
Dec	92	22	66,344	9.93	176
Dec	96	16	86,500	7.22	96

[a]BPV of hedged cash position divided by BPV of options (Option BPV equals futures BPV times put delta).
[b]Quantity of puts needed times price.
[c]BPV of futures expressed in percent of par times gamma times futures BPV in dollars, times quantity of puts used.
[d]Theta times $1,000 (1% of par) × quantity of puts used.

1. To minimize transaction costs, choose the put with the lowest quantity of contracts needed to hedge, the September 96 puts.
2. To get the most benefit from volatility, choose the contract which results in a hedge with the highest Δ BPV, the September 88 puts.
3. Choose the hedge with the lowest total time decay, the December 96 puts.
4. Choose the hedge which requires the least total premium up front, the September 88 puts.

Index

Add-on index pricing system, 48–49
Adjustable rate mortgage (ARM), 174–76
All-in cost (AIL), 101
American option, 108
Arbitrage, 18, 28–29
  cash and carry, 29–30
  constraints on option prices, 127–28
  measuring profit potential of, 32–34
  options, 144–46
  quasi-, 31–32
  reverse cash and carry, 30–31
Ascending-pennant formation, 211
Assets, creation of synthetic, 82–83
Asset value, protection of, 76–78

Balance sheet, rate sensitivity of, 11
Bar chart, in technical analysis, 209
Basic point value matching, 75–76
Basis, 34
  behavior over time, 35–40
Basis point, 57
Basis point value (BPV), 6
  advantages of, in rate risk management, 6–7
  extended applications of, 10–11
  limitations of, 11–12
  matching, 42–43, 75

and slope point value matched hedging, 89–92
using present value and yield to maturity to calaculate, for coupon security, 17
Bill basis, 34
Black, Fisher, 122
Black-Scholes model, 122–26, 137, 139
  versus reality, 148–50
Bond equivalent yield, 50–52
Box, 145
BPV. *See* Basic point value (BPV)
Break-even repo rate (BERR), 33
Brokers, 196
  expectations from, 206–7
Bucket, 206

Call option, 107
Caps, 182–83
Cash and carry arbitrage, 29–30
  reverse, 30–31
Cash flows, distinction between forwards versus futures, 23–24, 25
Centralization, distinction between forwards versus futures, 23, 25
Cheapness, importance of, in the futures market, 55–56
Chicago Board of Trade, regulatory activities of, 22

247